Misplaced

Misplaced

Colin P. Buckley

ധ๓ധ
Write My Wrongs

Write My Wrongs Co, United States

www.writemywrongs.co

Contents

Author's Note

My name is Colin Buckley, born Colin Patrick Brown. This story details my process through adoption, painful losses, and the effects of childhood trauma and abuse.

During my journey, I underwent many trials and tribulations, from my birth to becoming a victim of cult-like behavior modification programs and fighting for the freedom to form my own identity. My adoption story is not everyone's, but it is a cautionary tale, and it explains how genetics can play a bigger role than one might think. It warns parents with "troubled" teens to think twice, before sending your child away with the promise of a "cure."

Part 1

My mother had been gone for four days now. My grandparents were worried sick and had the police out looking for her.

She needed more clothes,
which meant she needed to go
back home to get them.

She walked through the door to find
only my grandmother home.
My grandfather was out searching for her.

Prior to my mother's return,
a family friend put a bug in
my grandmother's ear,
telling her my mother probably wasn't
coming home
because she was pregnant.

"You're not going anywhere!"
Yaya said,
stopping her rebellious
daughter from leaving again.
"Are you pregnant?"

"I don't know!" My mother answered,
sounding annoyed.

She thought she was grown
and knew it all.
How *dare* my grandmother
ask her such a question.

The next day, Yaya took my
13-year-old mother to
the hospital to have a
pregnancy test done, and
it was positive.

She was four months along already,
and having a boy.

That night, the family stood in the kitchen
to break the news to Grandfather
when he arrived home from work.

"Make her have an abortion,"
Grandfather ordered.
But Mother was too far along for that
to have been an option.

Grandfather was very much a manly man
in the 80s.
When it came to "girl problems,"
Yaya was the one who took care of it.

Mother's heart sank when she heard
his words.

She wanted her baby and
she knew if her father wanted this,
she wasn't going to be able to keep it.

She felt helpless.
This life was growing in her body and
she was not being given a say

During a doctor's visit,
my mother's nurse noticed the situation
and decided to bring in a binder of
couples looking to adopt.

The first couple to catch my mother's attention
lived on an eighty acre ranch and
were well off.

The second potential adoptees she found
were a couple who owned a pizzeria:
He couldn't have kids and she could.

Over the course of a week,
Mother had an interview
with the two couples.

She really liked the couple who owned the pizzeria.
They were kind. But
she really liked the wealthy couple who
lived on the ranch as well.

After a few more weeks,
Mother made her decision.

She decided she wanted everything.

Her baby could have the world with the
wealthy couple.
They had acreage, animals,
vehicles, and plenty to do.

Her baby would learn how to work
the farm, play in the mud,
and be able to go to college in the future.
They were perfect.

Until it came time to sign the papers.

When it came time for Mother to sign,
my new mom, Carole,
her real age was on the paper.

2/22/1937
She was 51 years old already.

They had lied.

"Nope!"
my mother said,
and refused to sign the paperwork.

Three weeks went by, filled with my
grandparent's attempts at getting
my mother to sign to no avail.

One day,
Grandfather approached my mother,
slid the papers to her,
and said,
"You're not taking this baby
away from those people,"
forcing her to sign.

Over the next couple of months,
Carole visited my mother periodically.
They went shopping together and
she bought her maternity clothes
once my mother began to show.

She grew to like Carole;
she thought she was a beautiful person.

Carole made up for the age discrepancy
with the woman she was.

***

Mother arrived at the hospital and was
assigned a room immediately.
The nurses attempted to
hook her up to IV's and give her medicine,
but she refused.

If I die during this birth,
at least I won't feel this pain anymore.
The now fourteen-year-old
thought to herself.

"If you're going natural,
You're going to need to sit up,"
one of the nurses ordered while she sat
my mother up in a squatting position.

After four hours of labor,
and forty-five minutes of pushing,
her baby was here.

Every time she held her newborn,
she didn't want to let him go.
This wasn't fair.
He was beautiful, perfect, and
he was supposed to be hers.

Every time she wasn't holding him,
she longed to have him in her arms.

The time finally came,
much too quickly, and
after two days,
mother and baby were released.

As she walked away from the hospital,
Auntie and Yaya each held an arm.

Mother turned around and

saw my father holding her newborn.
My strawberry blond hair was
glowing in the hospital lights.

She became overwhelmed with the
feelings of loss and emptiness.
It seemed like the hollowness was
swallowing her from the inside out,
causing tears to well in her eyes,
and she began to mourn.

3-15-89

Dear Brandy –

Just a note to see how you are doing & to reassure you that you are welcome to see Colin at any time in the future. The same for all of your family.

I know you are going through a rough time right now (remember I said it would get harder – not better) I wish you would consider counciling. We will be happy to pay for it. I feel it will help you alot right now – please let us know if we can help you in that area.

Colin is doing great – at least 15 lbs. I just bought him so darling clothes in size 6 mos. He was outgrowing everything!

Our love to you & your family.

Carol Buckley

3-15-89

Dear Brandy,

Just a note to see how you are doing and to reassure you that you are welcome to see Colin at any time in the future. The same for all of your family.

I know you are going through a rough time right now (remember I said it would get harder—not better). I wish you would consider counseling. We will be happy to pay for it. I feel it will help you a lot right now—please let us know if we can help you in that area.

Colin is doing great—at least 15 lbs. I just bought him some daily clothes size 6 months. He was outgrowing everything!

Our love to you and your family,
Carole Buckley

Part 2

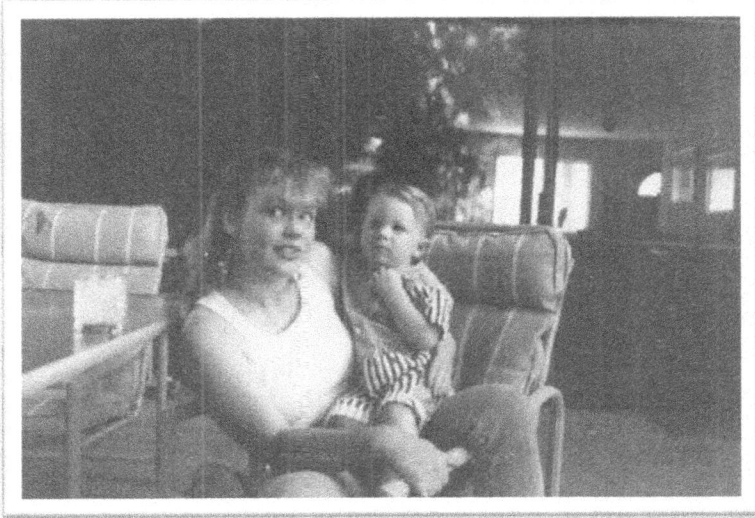

Mother and I during a visit.

Over the next couple of years,
Mother attempted to visit me when she could,
but Father was never too inviting.
While Mother would visit,
he always seemed antsy,
like the visit wasn't important or
like he was late to be somewhere.

One time, he even complained
to Grandfather about needing to get back
to work while Mother was
trying to spend time and
play with me.

Needless to say,
the visits from mother were few
because of the circumstances.

Nov. 30, 1993

Dear Shirley, brandy and all the Brown Family:

After your call on Conlin's birthday, I felt we
had better get a few things straightened out.

I did not mean to be rude to Brandy, but I could
not take a chance she would say "this is your mother".

Colin is an extremely well adjusted child and very
smart and we are gradually getting into the adoption
bit. But, we will do it our way. We do not want to
confuse him in any way.

He will know that he has a birth mother and father
when the time is right. Until then, I do not want
to confuse him.

If you want to visit or call you are welcome to at
any time, but not as his mother, grandmother, etc.
More as a friend for now.

When it is all worked out I will let you know and we
cn go from there.

Sincerely,

Carole Buckley

CAROLE BUCKLEY

***

"Daddy, can you push me?"
I asked Father,
my face pressed into the screen door.

We had a fun nightly routine
after our dinner settled.

Father put the newspaper down,
scooped me up,
and walked us over to the swing set.

I would squeal and laugh as
he pushed me higher and higher.

On the porch,
Mother would sit on the wooden bench
having a cigarette,
smiling as she watched us having fun.

The sunset turned the sky
purple and orange.

***

Mother and I bumped along the dirt road
in the family's old blue pickup;
an empty, ripped up dirt field was to our left.

Off in the distance, we could see Father
laying pipe in the ground.
It would eventually supply water
for future crops.

Upon arriving at the site,
I flipped my jacket inside out,
trying to trick Father into thinking I had
gotten a new jacket
without his knowledge.

I grabbed Father's lunch from the truck seat,
flung open the door,
and ran as fast as my little legs would carry me
to give Father his midday
meal.

He picked me up and
laughed at my inside out jacket.

The trick hadn't worked out,
but we still had a laugh at the attempt.

As Mother and I drove from the site,
I was already thinking of mine and Father's
evening swing set time.

***

Sometimes, when we weren't in a hurry,
Father would place me on his lap
and let me steer.
My feet couldn't reach the pedals yet.

I loved it when he let me drive.

I would cruise down the quarter mile
long driveway
and down two stretches of country road
before coming to the main road.

Still, to this day, I can't remember
not knowing how to drive.

Misplaced

I brought my shoe over to the bed,
and Mother showed me
how to tie my shoelaces
once again.

I took the shoe back
and tied the simple knot,
but looser than hers.

She smiled and clapped
for my little milestone.

I tied my shoes
all on my own.

One of our last moments together.

***

I watched from the doorway as
Father approached
Mother in bed.

He had paperwork for her to sign,
but she was too weak to hold the pen—
the cancer's toll.

He cupped his hand around hers
to help her sign.

I wouldn't know the significance of this,
until later in life.

***

Father sat in the reading lounge
and summoned me over to him.

"Mommy died,"
he informed me
as heartbroken tears
rolled down his face.

Gesturing to me,
he stood up and
we began walking to the bedroom,
where Mother lay resting.

I couldn't comprehend
what I was seeing:
her eyes, closed,
mouth, slightly open,
and she was laying breathlessly still.

I was too scared to hold Mother's hand,
as Father had coaxed.
I backed away, crying instead.

I had never seen death before.
I was only five years old.

I left the bedroom that day,
unaware that the course of my life
had been drastically
altered.

Part 3

T he world seemed still.
Most of my days were
spent with a sitter.

Sometimes,
after Father arrived home from work,
we threw a football back and forth.

Father had just finished building our big,
beautiful new ranch home,
and the living room was big enough
for the simple game.
My new room was upstairs and on the
opposite corner of the house
from Father's room.

I had to walk down the stairs,
across the living room, and
through a skyway office that
used to be my room
to get there now.

Most nights for dinner we had hotdogs
or other things not requiring much preparation.
Father wasn't much of a cook,
but at five years old I didn't mind it.

***

I swung on the swings
and
slid down the slides.
I ran around aimlessly,
as little kids do.

Just off to the side of the playground,
Father chatted with a woman
beneath a tree.

He called and gestured for
me to come join them.

He introduced the woman to me,
and asked what I thought
of the woman coming to live with us.

In my innocence,
I smiled and said, "Ya."

The woman and I
chatted for a while longer.
She had four children of her own:
two boys and two girls.
Micah, the oldest;
Norma, the oldest girl,
Nathan, the second youngest;
and Rachel, the youngest.

"Are they nice?"
I asked the woman
as she spoke of my future siblings.

Although I missed Mother terribly,
I became excited
at the thought of having a big,
new family.

***

As we pulled into the driveway,
I turned around in my seat
to look at Nathan.
"I'm adopted." I proclaimed,
smiling.

He looked stunned
and laughed a little.
"Do you know what that means?"
he asked me.

As my brother explained what it meant,
I listened,
learning and becoming aware
of the definition of the word.

Prior to this engagement,
I knew I was adopted,
but I never knew what it meant.
I never understood the meaning
behind the word.

But now I did.
My dad was not my real dad,
and Mother had not been my real mother.

***

I was six years old.
Mother had passed.
I found out what adoption truly meant,
and I had gained an entirely new family,
all in six months' time.

I had gone from being the only one,
to one of four.

As time went on,
my grades began to suffer
and my behavior changed.

Instead of seeking help for me,
Father bared down.
He began dictating my every move.

I believe he thought discipline would "fix" me.

My mother was gone,
and I just needed a dad.

My siblings did well in school.
Rachel, especially.
She was on the honor roll and
received nothing short of perfect marks.

I was often compared to them
during my many reprimands.
A definitive line was established
between my siblings and I,
as their mom could act as a barrier to
my father's rage.

I began calling her "Mom" quickly.
I was young and my siblings called her mom.
I knew she cared for me
and it seemed natural.

However,
my siblings were Mom's children,
and I was my father's to deal with.

Aside from the normal sibling rivalries,
I enjoyed having a brother
and sisters.

I wasn't alone anymore.

I grew close to Rachel,
who was closest to my age,
and Nathan, who was a couple years older.

Rachel was artistic and caring while
Nathan introduced me to skateboarding,
fishing,
and rock music.

I grew close with Norma as well,
but she played more of a big sister roll
to me,
as she was middle school aged already.

I enjoyed my new family,
but my interactions with Father became
surface level at best.

It was as if, as I got older,
my dad from the swing set
grew further away from me.

It was either discipline,
arguing over the night's homework,
or questions challenging my intelligence.
Very rarely did I catch a smile
from Father,
and when I did,
it was at my expense.

All the wooden spoons in the house were broken;
only the thickest spoon remained.
On the bad days,
Mom would hide the spoon,
anticipating his harsh reprimands—
her quiet protest against his idea of discipline.

Father believed I should remain in trouble
until my grades came up,
and my behavior became better.

But in his version of trouble,
I wasn't worthy of kindness,
compassion, or love.

Part 4

I started asking about my "real mom"
rather frequently.
It was an open adoption, and
my curiosity was piqued.

With the loss of my mother
and the lack of nurturing from my father,
was I seeking comfort?
Answers?

I never felt like I fit into my father's box,
or the idea of who he thought I should be.
Would I fit in with her?

I asked Father for her number,
but he said he didn't know.

Then, in one of her few silent protests,
Mom slapped a sticky note on the kitchen table
where Mother's name and phone number were written.
Seeing the name,
a lump formed in my throat.

I was nervous,
not knowing what I would say.

I hesitated before picking up the landline's receiver
and dialed the scribbled number.

After a couple of rings,
an older woman answered,
it was my grandmother.
I introduced myself,
and then asked for my mother
by name.
She picked up the receiver,
already in tears.
"Hi baby!"

"Do you have big hands?"
she asked
through an obvious, teary smile.
Her expressions were
noticeable through the phone;
I could picture her smile.

"Not really," I replied.
I was overwhelmed with nerves and
didn't quite know what to say.

I couldn't process the idea
of someone being so happy to speak to me
that they cried.

No one had ever taken such an
interest in me.
The questions seemed odd.

I had grandparents
and two brothers I had never met:
Jared and Larry.
I also found out my bio dad
died by suicide when I was a year old.

Another death…
It seemed appropriate.

The hope of another dad,
snuffed out.

My world was spinning.
It was like there was another world.
Another life.

I thought of this life often.

Where the phrase,
"Kids will be kids" was used
and not,
"Kids are meant to be seen
not heard."

It gave me a little peace
during the bleak
monotonous chores
and my father's disappointment.

***

I knocked on the door and within a
couple of seconds,
found myself in the biggest,
warmest hug I had ever gotten.
Mother was crying,
and left tears on my cheek
when she pulled back.

I had never received a hug that big
and warm.
No one had ever been so happy and
excited to see me.

My brothers and cousins and
I played in the park.

We liked the same shows,
laughed at the same things,
and had the same interests.

We finished each other's sentences
and had the same ideas.

We were all
alike.

Was this what a family was
supposed to feel like?
Was this what I had been missing out on?

They loved each other and
cared for each other...
and I was included.

Being adopted,
I had never experienced a closeness
like this;
never felt a sense of belonging.

It was like I had been
misunderstood my whole life.

I had no one who related to me,
and no one I related to.
No one ever understood where I was coming from.
It was like there had always been a void
and I didn't know it.

I always felt like a fish out of water
but now, I didn't.

During this visit with my family,
I finally felt
home.

Part 5

N athan got a go cart as a birthday gift.
Father thought it would be good
transportation for his river trips.

Nathan liked to go to the river to fish.

I would stand on the back
of the little go cart
while my brother drove through the
orchards,
sometimes going to the river,
and sometimes driving around aimlessly.

I think I liked the go cart just
as much as Nathan,
if not more,
even though I wasn't tall enough to
reach the pedals.

It had become an escape from the house,
and a way to get out from under my
father's watchful eye.
I would try to avoid him

at all costs.
If I was caught trying to have fun,
he would put me to work.

***

Father purchased time shares,
and the family took annual trips to Hawaii.
One year, we even spent a week in Paris,
where we saw the Eiffel Tower
and visited various museums;
we even saw the Mona Lisa.

These times were somewhat
of a break for me.
Father didn't have many expectations
while we were on vacation.
Although I remained under his thumb,
more so because we were away
and there were no escapes,
there weren't many times I found myself in trouble
while we were in public or on vacation.

"Children are meant to be seen,
not heard,"
was preached.

As an eight-year-old,
that was a difficult philosophy to live up to,
so, there were still moments on vacation
I found myself at the mercy of Father's hand.

It just happened less frequently.

***

I could feel the anxiety in my chest as
I clung to the rope.
My feet were wet and
it felt like I could
slip at any moment.

I waited for the person in the
water below to swim out of the way and
then I jumped.

The wind swooshed by my ears as
I clung to the rope with everything I had,
until my outward swing peaked, and
I let go, flinging myself forward through the air.

I managed to complete my flip
just in time to hit the water right side up.
But instead of hitting feet first,
I hit the backs of my thighs with a loud
SMACK.

"Ooooh!"
my brother and sisters exclaimed.

Kauai had become our "go to"
annual vacation spot and
we learned the island pretty well.

We ended up finding this little cove that
only the locals knew of.
It had a waterfall and a big rope swing that
hung from a big, old native tree.
The tree's roots clung to the rock face
all the way down to the water.
We used them to climb out of the water and
set up for the rope swing again.

It was a beautiful spot, and

it was where I was actually able to let loose.
I was able to have some fun and be a kid.
It was easily my favorite place in the world
at the time.

***

We were all loaded in the car…
waiting for Father to finish his last few tasks for
work before the weekend.

He had stopped by the car and
put his Gatorade in the cup holder and
then taken off again to do
one last thing.

Nathan grabbed his Gatorade and
started drinking it.
Then he handed it to me.

"Hurry before he gets back!" he said in
a rushed toned.

I chugged what I could and
gave the bottle back to Nathan to
finish.

Once he was done,
he placed the bottle between my legs
right as Father got into the car.
"Is that my Gatorade?"
Father asked.
"Ya," I answered nervously.

He snatched the empty bottle from my lap and
threw it angrily against the dashboard of the car.

"Fuck!" he yelled, and
then picked the bottle up and
threw it at the dash one last time.

"What is wrong with you?" Mom asked,
looking appalled.

"I've been working all morning and I'm thirsty!" he answered, his voice still raised.

"That was ridiculous," Mom said to him
as he stepped out of the car to get another one.

Nathan and I looked at each other with wide eyes and
tried our best to not laugh at the
complete fit my father threw.

Even though Nathan
set me up for failure,
by placing the bottle in my lap instead of
back in the cup holder,
it was always fun when we teamed up.

***

I was asleep in bed
when my door suddenly burst open.
Startled, I lifted my head.
Through my blurred vision,
I could see it was Nathan.

"See! He's not even asleep!
"He's the devil!"
he yelled, then vanished as
quickly as he had appeared.

My oldest sister, Norma
came to the door,
telling me not to worry
and to go back to sleep.

Of course, my curiosity
wouldn't let me do as my sister said.
As soon as she left,
I jumped from my bed and ran
to peek from the door.

This was the first time
I had seen my brother this way.
I knew of his ailments,
and had been to the hospital to visit him before,
but I had never witnessed one of his episodes.

By this time, Nathan
wasn't well enough to attend school,
and spent most of his days with Mom
or Father.

The episodes started happening
right around the time of
his Bar Mitzvah.

Almost every day, Nathan would come downstairs

already dressed in riding pants,
ready to go with Mom on her daily horse ride.
If there was no horse riding that day,
he would go to work with Father,
putting in irrigation systems for other farms.

This episode became too much
for the family to handle on their own,
and Mom was forced
to make the difficult decision of contacting the police
and having Nathan taken
back to the hospital.

I was always saddened,
and the house always felt a little empty
while he was away.

***

It was the day of love:
Valentine's day.

Micah had driven in
from the bay the night before,
and taken Nathan
snowboarding for the day.

They were both good at
various sports and frequented
California ski resorts often.

I was often left out of these outings
because I was too young—
only nine.

The family was sitting watching TV
when Micah returned,
looking distraught.
Without saying anything,
he sat on the couch,
tears slowly rolling down his cheeks.

"I don't know how to say this,"
he said,
nearly choking on his words.
"Nathan died."

His words instantly sent Mom into hysterics.
She let out a cry I had never heard before.
The sound was indescribable, utter grief.

Not knowing how to cope,
and overwhelmed by the pain on everyone's faces,
Mom, Dad, Rachel, and Micah's.
The weight of the scene that was unfolding,
the noises all blurring into one.
I ran upstairs.

"I will always be here for you,"
as I spoke to him in my room.

Norma was at her friend's house,
which meant Father and I had to go pick her up.

After she settled in the car,
Father spoke first.
"Something happened," he said.

***

Nathan's accident took place at a
major ski resort.

The newspaper called in less than twenty-four hours.
As much as we wanted privacy,
they wanted their story.

Thirteen-year-old Dies Tragically

"Write whatever you want."
Father told them,
as he hung up the receiver appalled.

In the days that followed,
adults made plans,
and my family was again
buried in grief.

Misplaced

Just three years after my mother passed,
death was becoming familiar.

It was odd that at thirteen years old,
my brother knew what he wanted in death.

He always said if he were to die,
he wanted to be buried near water,
with a fishing pole stuck in the ground
so he could fish forever.

My brother was buried near the family's pond,
under the old willow tree,
fishing lures and his favorite
glass bottled coke decorated the
thirteen-year-old's burial site.

Part 6

I had been assigned the task of
pulling weeds out in front of the house.
I was to start the next morning.

We had a big circular driveway
with a pond and flowerbeds.
The job would easily take me all week.

I was only eleven.

I didn't think it was fair of Father
to ask that of me;
Jared, my biological brother, was visiting.
What would my brother do while I worked all day?
I didn't want to ask him to help me work.
That's not what he came to visit for.

The next morning, we woke
without a care in the world
and went about our daily routine
of fun activities.

Father arrived home that afternoon

to find the two of us swimming in the pool
in our underwear.

The task from the night before?
Not even started.

He walked over to us
and asked me why the job
hadn't been completed.

I gasped, realizing my fault,
and told him I had forgotten.

"Get out and meet me out front,"
he ordered.

I knew I was in trouble.

When I approached Father,
I wasn't given a chance to speak.
He grabbed me and threw me into the fence
bordering one of the flower beds,
and started hitting me.

All I could do was cover my head with my arms
in an attempt to protect myself.
The blows hit me everywhere,
up and down my torso,
lasting long enough for me to
actually wonder
when it was going to stop.

The wailing finally ceased,
but only so he could scream
in my face.

While Father yelled,
he pointed and shook his finger.
For some reason, it
overwhelmed me with a

sense of annoyance.
I tried to move it away from my face
by pushing Father's hand away.

That was a mistake.

He began hitting me again.
This time the blows only ceased
because I had fallen to the dirt.

"Now you stay here and do what you're told!
"I want it perfect!"
he yelled at me while I laid in the dirt,
crying
and trying to regain my breath.

As Father walked away,
I cried to him, asking if I could get dressed.
I was still in my underwear from swimming.
My question was met with an abrupt,
"No!"

I felt defeated and
didn't know what to do.

I rolled over
to my hands and knees and
noticed a cut on my hand from the fence.

I chewed some of the ripped,
loose flesh from it out of habit,
and began Father's assignment.

Vehicles of crew members
and delivery drivers all
drove by me while I was out there
working in my underwear.

I felt embarrassed and
humiliated,

but there was nothing I could do.

I didn't know what he would do if I
disobeyed him by trying to sneak into the house
to get my clothes.

***

Mom was walking across the living room
with a pistol in her back pocket
and a glass of wine in her hand.
Father was in close pursuit of his
obviously intoxicated wife.

"She has a gun," Father said as he noticed
me watching from the balcony.

I watched as Mom entered the kitchen
to top off her glass of wine.
Just as she attempted to pour the bottle,
Father slid over the countertop on his stomach
and snatched the weapon from her pocket.

"I got it," he called up to me.

After some bickering between the two,
Father coaxed and began herding
her toward their bedroom.
As they made their way,
I walked downstairs.
Father informed me of a second weapon
located in Mom's nightstand.
I ran ahead of my two arguing parents
and grabbed the revolver from her nightstand.

"Your derelict kid has my gun,"
she drunkenly slurred
as I made way out of the room.

Shrugging off the remark,
I stood and waited for Father to come out,
and gave him the gun.

The next day, Mom told me
Father had "gotten his dick sucked,"
while he and I stayed the night at a friend's house

for New Years.

Later in life, I learned
the friend accused him of rape.
She claimed Father had
forced himself on top of her.
There were never charges received because
they had both been drinking that night
and had conflicting stories.

***

"How come you decided to pick me up today?" I asked.

"I don't want you doing anything you want to do!"
Father answered.

Earlier in the day I had received a
referral from the teacher for talking in class.
While in summer school,
we were only allowed to receive two referrals, and
if we did, we were kicked out and
had to repeat the grade.

This was seventh grade middle school, and
the rules were a little stricter.

I had received one referral now.

Even so, it wasn't like Father to pick me up.
Normally I would wait till I got home to receive
my reprimands.

I think he was under the impression
I enjoyed riding the bus.
So, instead of letting me ride the bus,
he picked me up.

I didn't enjoy the bus.
I just rode it because I had to, and
I simultaneously didn't mind.

"You got in trouble for TALKING!" he screamed
as he slammed his hands on the wheel repeatedly.

"When we get home,
I'm whoopin your ass!" he yelled.

He was screaming so loudly in the
enclosed vehicle, the sound seemed to

reverberate and it became overwhelming so,
I began to cry.
"Ok." I muttered, and then sat silently.

I was hoping if I didn't say
anything for the rest of the ride,
he would calm down a little and
my punishment may not be as severe.
I even tried to muffle my sniffles but,

I was wrong.

We pulled into the carport, and he got out,
slamming his door in the process.
I only got my door halfway open before
he yanked it open and pulled me from the car.

In one swift movement he pulled me from the car,
threw me into the front door of the house and
began hitting me.
I covered my head to protect myself while the
blows landed everywhere up and down my torso.

I couldn't go anywhere with my back against the door.
It was like I was a ball bouncing between the
paws of some big, dumb, angry bear.

Finally, I collapsed onto the door mat,
fighting to catch my breath.

Without saying anything,
he stepped over me and walked into the house,
slamming the door behind him.

Why did I keep messing up?
I'm *stupid.*
I hate myself
Why can't I just be normal?

I caught my breathe and let out a

scream of rage and frustration.

Just then the door behind me opened and
I caught a couple more blows from Father.
"You out here screamin'!?" he yelled as he towered over me,
inches from my face.
"Be quiet!" he yelled before
slamming the door closed again.

After a couple minutes,
I wiped my face, picked up my backpack, and
walked to my room,
hoping to miss Father on the way.

***

"How was school?"
Father asked.

It was the question that started almost every
nightly argument.
Even so,
he still asked every night.

"I don't want to talk about it."

"Why?" Father asked.
His tone was stern, and his voice had
already begun to raise.
"It'll just piss me off," I responded.

As I completed that sentence,
he pushed me off my stool
into the living room.
"You wanna fight!?"
Father screamed as he walked toward me.

I managed to stand up
just in time to receive another shove
to my chest.
"Come on, let's fight!"
"Let's fight!"
"Let's fight!"
he yelled each time he pushed me.

Finally, I was able to regain my balance,
and as I did,
I grabbed two handfuls of Father's shirt
and pushed with everything I had.

I drove him across the living room,
all the way to where the family's grand piano sat,
and slammed him into it.

For a split second, I thought I might
have the upper hand in this fight.

But then Father picked me up
and ran across the living room.
When we reached the other side, he
slammed me into the wall
between two windows.

After he was done yelling in my face,
he made me sit back down at the dinner table
and tell him what happened at school that day,
which had been nothing.

The day had been uneventful.

I just associated the question with
altercations between Father and I.

I didn't want to talk about my school day
because Father was in the habit of
picking apart everything I told him,
and I feared he would find something to
get on me about.

I gave that answer because
I was trying to avoid a fight.

The next day I woke
with my back hurting.
I walked to the mirror and
lifted my shirt to reveal a
bruise on each of my shoulder blades,
where Father had slammed me
into the trim between the two windows.

Part 7

I didn't do well in school.
I was always hyper and messing around,
and my focus was on fun rather than work.

I couldn't have fun at home,
so school was my only outlet.
At least school didn't hit me as a
form of punishment.

Instead of trying to find out why I was
acting out and doing poorly,
Father thought I should be in trouble
until I improved,

I was living under an abusive dictator.

Every time I was in trouble,
the punishment never
fit the crime.

It was much worse.

"The punishment has to be so severe
that he never wants to do it again."

I couldn't wear the clothes I wanted,
I couldn't style my hair how I wanted,
and I couldn't listen to the music I enjoyed.
I had no bodily autonomy,
robbed of any chance at forming
my own identity.
With this, my anger and depression grew.

I watched from the sidelines as my sister Rachel,
was able to live her childhood.
(Norma had already moved out,
overwhelmed by the household dynamics.)
My brain fixated on why I couldn't have
my own childhood.

I was used as free labor.
It was like my father had the thought to
adopt and raise an employee rather than a son
an employee he was never happy with.

Or maybe, when Mother died,
he became stuck with a child he
never wanted in the first place.

He held me to adult standards
as soon as I reached age eleven,
so nothing was ever good enough.
The feeling of defeat never ceased.

Father was impossible to please:
always demanding perfection.

I finally managed to fight enough,
talk about it enough, and ask enough
that Father let me go live with my
biological family
when I was fourteen.

I broke an adoption I didn't want
because I never felt wanted.

***

I wandered around campus alone
and somewhat nervous.
I was new to the school and didn't know how to
make friends.

I could see the group of kids
I wanted to hang out with.
They wore rock and metal band shirts.
I knew we at least had the same music tastes,
and I found that group to be the type of
people I generally got along with,
but I didn't know how to talk to them
or break the ice, so to speak.
So, I walked around by myself
until the bell rang.

But I was happy.

I couldn't wait to get home from school,
when before I used to dread it.
I believe my father thought I wasn't going to
like it at my mother's because the
quality of life seemed lower to him.
But to me,
the quality of life was better.
I would rather live how I was and
wander around school with no friends
than live in my father's house.

We lived in a single wide trailer, and
most nights I would sleep on the couch,
or I would sleep on the floor in my brothers'
room.
Even though Mother didn't have a lot of money,
she had a lot of love to give,
and I was accepted.

I belonged.

When Mother got home from work, she
greeted my brothers and I with hugs.

When she asked how my day went,
it didn't result in confrontation.

I was allowed to wear what I wanted,
and listen to the music I liked.
My brothers were my friends and
we were allowed to go to people's houses
and play video games if we wanted to.

I could sleep in on the weekends,
and I was allowed to be a kid.

My grades were finally good and
I wasn't getting in trouble at school anymore.

Schoolwork seemed easier.
It's amazing how easy learning becomes
when you're truly happy.

I was floating.
I was part of a family of five,
who all loved and cared for each other.

Finally,
at fourteen years old,
I could relax without worrying when the next fight
would break out, or worrying about what my father
was going to be disappointed about next.

***

"Hi number one," Yaya would say as I walked
through the door.

She always greeted all of us at the door with a
hug and a kiss.
We would go to her house quite frequently,
as she only lived five minutes away.
Sometimes, when my brothers and I were out
romping around the neighborhood on our bikes and
skateboards,
we would stop in just to say hello.

"You know, I could kick myself for
throwing that letter away," Yaya said.

Every time we came over to Yaya and Grandfather's
house, Yaya always told us family history and
old stories of us when we were younger.

This time she was talking about a letter
Carole, my mother who adopted me,
had written.

Back when Carole was sick, she had apparently
written a letter to Mother.

In it,
she wrote of her ailments and
told Yaya, Grandfather, and Mother not to worry.
If she were to succumb to the sickness,
there was a hefty life insurance policy I
would have access to when I reached the rightful
age of twenty-five.

I was going to be okay if she passed on.

"It's okay, Yaya," I said. "It's probably already
gone. Father probably won't ever give it to me,

anyway."

I hoped I was wrong when I said that,
but I knew I was probably right.
Remembering the moment my father
was *helping* Carole sign papers
on her death bed.

Part 8

S chool ended, and
I received a call from Father.
Even though he had let me live
with Mother,
he still wanted to see me.

He even invited my brother to come along.

The visit was going surprisingly well.
Jared and I romped around on the farm,
swam in the pool,
and had lots of fun.

Father and I hadn't argued at all.

One afternoon, Father stopped my brother and I
in front of the house as we were running around.
He told Jared that he was going back to
Mother's in the morning,
and that he should probably start packing his things.

"When am I going back?" I asked Father.

That's when he said the
last thing I ever wanted to hear.

"You're not going back."

God damn, those words echoed.

He wasn't letting me go back to Mother's.
He was forcing me to stay with him.

I didn't understand.

I was doing well in school.
I had finally made friends.
I had a girlfriend,
a life,
my mother,
brothers,
cousins,
my grandparents;
I had built a whole world—
a whole life I loved and
was happy in,
and it was all being ripped away from me.

With Father, I couldn't wear what I wanted,
I couldn't listen to the music I liked.
I couldn't go to friend's houses.
I had to work on the weekends.
I had to work during the summers.
He yelled at me and hit me
when I got in trouble.
He was mean to me,
and I never even knew why.

For some reason,
he wanted me to live with him,
but he treated me like he
couldn't stand having me around;

like I was a nuisance.

I was devastated by the news.
When I asked why,
he told me he thought
it was better for me to stay with him.

It wasn't even a reason I understood.

My heart sank in my chest.
I had thoughts of running away to
Mother's.
But then he would just come get me.
There was nothing Mother could do,
since legally,
Father had adopted me fifteen years ago,
and I belonged to him.

I was stuck.

Part 9

I couldn't take it anymore.
I hated living there
and needed to leave.

I pulled down my sister Norma's old Raleigh
that she had left behind
and fixed it up.

Then I made a call to the bus station,
retrieved everything I needed
to purchase a ticket to Reno,
and packed a bag.

I just needed to wait for nightfall,
and I could begin my journey.
Lucky for me,
Mom and Father retired early most nights.

After I saw the glow of the
living room lights disappear
from under my door,
I slowly peaked out to make sure

the coast was clear.
I watched as Father walked through the office and
into his bedroom.
I made my way down the hallway,
and out the front door.

As I made my way down the driveway on the bicycle,
I had never been more nervous in my life.
I knew where the bus station was,
and the route was a two-lane country road.
A child on a bike in the middle of the night
would stick out like a sore thumb to any patrolling police.
Even when I reached the city,
I would still be out of place
because of how young I was
and the hour.

But it was a risk worth taking.
I was prepared to take any
punishment administered by Father.

This was my happiness and freedom I was running for.

I made my way to the main road and
turned left to head toward the city.
As I made my way down the road,
I came upon another man on a bicycle.
For a while, I trailed the man,
maintaining a decent distance.

This was a stranger in the middle of the night,
and I didn't want to draw attention to myself.

But it didn't work.
Once the man turned around to
check over his shoulder,
he saw me and slowed down.

"Where you headed?" he asked me.
"The bus station."

"You know how to get there?"
"Ya," I said. "Do you know what time it opens?"
"I think around six," the man answered.

He was tall and slim.
He had a grungy backpack and
an old, weathered beanie on his head.

We pedaled down the road a little while longer
and eventually turned into a col-de-sac
to take a short break.
While we were stopped,
I reached into my backpack to
grab my wallet chain,
and put it on.

"I ain't gonna hurt you, kid," the man said
as he took a drag from his cigarette.

I didn't say anything because
I wanted him to believe I remained wary.
But I didn't attach the chain to have
a weapon at the ready.
I attached the chain,
excited to be able to wear it.

"It makes you look like a gangster,"
Father would say.

We started riding again,
making small talk along the way.
I ended up asking where he lived and
that's when I learned the man was homeless.
The tattered clothing kind of told me that,
but I asked anyway, just in case.

All he had to his name
was what was in his backpack and
the bike he was riding.

We made it to the city and
the man asked if I was
used to being around drugs,
because if I was,
he knew where we could crash for the night.

I told him that I wasn't. I was fifteen and
growing up with rich people in seclusion.

"Okay, I just need to make a stop,
and then we can keep goin',"
he said to me.

We left our route for only a minute to stop
at a smaller town home with an overgrown front lawn.

"I got a fuckin' runaway tonight,"
I overheard as he walked through the door.

After a couple of minutes, he came back out and
we started down the road again.

We arrived at the greyhound station,
but it was too early and
it wasn't open yet.

Just down the road, there was a grape vineyard
we decided to make our home for the night.
We made our way far enough in to be
out of sight of passersby.

As we hunkered down,
the man hugged himself and asked,
"You got another one of those?"
as he pointed to the sweater I was wearing.

I reached into my backpack and
pulled out the spare one I had packed myself and
gave it to him.

We laid in the dirt of the vineyard
attempting to catch some sleep, to no avail.
It was chilly that night and
I was too anxious about the adventure I was on
to be able to sleep.

After a while, I could see the sun start to rise and
knew it was almost time for the bus station to open.

As we stood up, the man
handed me my sweater back, saying,
"I sure could use one of those."

I wanted to give this man my sweater.
He had helped me through the night.
He gave up a warm place to sleep to
make sure I got to the bus station okay.

But I didn't.

Mom and Father had taught me to
never give the homeless anything
because they would just spend it on drugs.
so, I didn't think I should give it to him,

even though I wanted to.

I didn't think it was right to give it to him,
even though I felt it was.

We made our way out of the vineyard and
finally to the bus station,
where we said our good lucks and
I boarded the first bus to Reno.

***

To the homeless man who helped me:

Thank you for keeping me company and making sure I made it to the bus station that night. I'm sorry for not giving you my spare sweater, it's a memory that still haunts me. I wish I could go back and make it right. You kept me safe. My story might have ended that night, had you been someone else. I was raised to place judgement on people in your circumstance. I wasn't taught much compassion or empathy. Something that I didn't learn until much later in life. That's not an excuse, just how I was raised, and I was a confused boy. I hope life eventually dealt you some decent cards. You probably won't see this, but just know I am eternally grateful to you.

Until we meet again.

***

I had to change buses when
we got to Sacramento.

It was only about a twenty-minute layover,
but for a fifteen-year-old runaway,
it seemed like an eternity.

I was nervous;
anxious.

I stood in line, keeping a wary eye on
everyone and everything around me.

Two police officers walked into the bus station
with dogs,
and my heart skipped a beat.

I thought my dad noticed I was
gone already.

The line I was standing in was
on the opposite side of the lobby
from where the dogs were.
I didn't want to talk to the police.
I didn't want to answer any questions.

What if they were actually looking for me
because my father called them?

They made it about halfway across the lobby
and then my line began to move.

I could feel my heart start to slow down.

I handed the man at the door my ticket and
boarded the final bus to Reno.

***

I stepped off the bus and felt liberated;
I felt at home stepping foot on the familiar
sidewalks of the city.
I had successfully made it
all the way from Modesto, CA
to Reno, NV.

It was exhilarating.

But as happy and excited as I was,
I came to the realization that I couldn't
go straight to my mother's house
like I wanted to.

I didn't know if Father had discovered I was gone yet,
and I didn't know if my mother was going to be forced to
call the police upon my arrival.

So, I decided to go to my girlfriend's house first.

I could at least see her for a little while and
try to come up with a plan for every scenario
I could think of before I went to my mother's.
Her parents were at work,
so, she was the one who answered the door.
We went straight to her room to hide me
because her parents would be home any minute.

We tried to come up with a plan
to no avail.
She ended up grabbing her dinner and telling
her parents she wanted to eat in her room,
so I could have the first thing I had eaten in
twenty-four hours.

We shared her dinner and
ended up falling asleep for the night.

I woke the next morning to a
big crash and
commotion outside.

I opened my eyes to see my
girlfriend walking back into her
room looking fearful.

It was Mother.
When I walked outside,
she gave me one of her big "mom hugs" and
started crying.
She couldn't believe I was there, and
she was happy I was safe.

Apparently, she had ripped their shed door open
my girlfriend's family hadn't been able to unstick for
quite some time.

My father hadn't noticed I was missing until
eight o'clock at night, and
that's when he called her.

I was supposed to be working in the orchard
on the farm,
and he thought I had gotten up early to
beat the summer heat.

In reality,
I was already at the bus station.

We got in the car, and she took me
straight to my grandmother's house.
When we got there,
Yaya made me a big breakfast
and we chatted about my journey.
The whole time I was telling my story,
she stared at me, smiling and with
tears in her eyes.
Mother agreed to give me the rest of the day

before she called my father.
She had to call him
because the police were looking for me.

I was bummed, but hopeful.

Maybe this would show Father
how much I wanted to live there.
Maybe it would show him how much I wanted
to be with my family;
my family who showed me love, compassion, and
understood me.

Hopefully, this would show
him that this was what I truly wanted,
and hopefully, he would honor my wishes.

Mother got off the phone that evening
and explained to me Father would be there
the following day to pick me up.

I was heartbroken.

To be honest,
I didn't know how much longer
I could go on like that.
A thought, that scared me.

How could I continue to live
as a prisoner of my father's?

My brother and I stayed up late that night,
scheming of ways to get me to stay.
While we were talking, my girlfriend
showed up.
She told me we could run again and
she had a place we could stay in the city.
One of her friend's parents was gone.

I turned to Jared and asked if he wanted to come,

but he said no.
This was the only option I saw.
Maybe I could force my stay there in Reno and
remain with my family

I could go on the run again and
stay gone until I knew Father
had come and gone.
I knew he wouldn't hang around
in Reno long.
Especially with my mother.

That was the new plan.

As soon as I left Mother's,
we headed for the hills
surrounding the trailer park.

My girlfriend and I reached a spot in the hills where
I could look down and see Mother's trailer.
I saw lights and a car leaving the driveway,
so I knew Jared had told mother that I left.

He had done what he said he was going to do though,
and given us a head start.
We walked through the hills
toward the city, in the dark,
for what seemed like hours.
We reached pavement and
made our way to the townhomes,
and finally reached the place.
Her friend let us in and
led us down to the basement.

We fell asleep and woke up
sometime in the afternoon.
We had been exhausted from our adventure
the night before.

We all hung out and waited until nightfall

before I used the house phone
to call Mother.

My father had come and gone,
like I thought he would.
I told my mother where I was
and she came to pick us up.

When we got home,
we had a sit down and
she explained I was going to have to go back
to Father's house.
There was nothing she could do about it,
and she had to put me on the bus in the morning.
Her hands were tied.

I was sad and heartbroken, and I knew
I had to give up.

I wasn't going to be able to live with my mother.
I was going to be stuck with Father for
at least the next two and a half years,
and there was nothing anyone could do
to help me.

Part 10

"Hey, wake up! Get ready to go,"
Father said.

I worked my eyes open and
saw him standing there in my doorway.

"I don't want to go," I moaned.
"I know, but it's good for you. Get up and
meet me out front," he ordered.

I did not want to go to work with him today.
I was tired of going with him only to get
yelled at because everything I did was
unsatisfactory to him.

I wanted to have a normal weekend and
maybe hang out with my friends for once.
A luxury that was only awarded to me
on the rare occasion Father was pleased
with me, or didn't have the patience to
deal with me.

I lazily sat up in bed and
began to get dressed,
but then quickly decided,
no.

I wasn't going to work this weekend away.
It wasn't fair that my sister got to do what she wanted,
my friends all got to do what they wanted,
but I never got to.
Why wasn't I allowed to be a kid?

So I sat on my bed and waited.

Finally, after a few minutes,
he came back into my room to get me and
I wouldn't budge.
I threw my argument at him, but
he didn't want to hear it.

"Let's go, right now," he ordered.
"No!" I yelled back.

That's when he came into my room and
disconnected my phone.

He knew that was the only thing I had to
keep in contact with my mom and
the rest of my biological family, and
he knew that's how he could hurt me the most
for disobeying him.

I quickly jumped up,
grabbed the cord of the phone, and
wrapped it around my hand several times to
secure my grasp.

"Let go of the phone!" he yelled.

But I stood my ground.

I wasn't going to let this
big, bumbling idiot
sever the only line of communication
I had with my family.

Then he yanked the phone away,
snapping the cord.

He walked away with the phone.
While I stood, dumbfounded,
the snapped cord still in my hand.

That sent me into a rage.
I slammed my door and
screamed with everything I had.

I was furious.
Why me?
Why was I the only one
he dictated and tormented?
I hated it there, and for some reason,
he was keeping me there.
I felt powerless, helpless, and
I hated him.

***

I stepped off the school bus
and started my walk
down the long gravel driveway,
flinching and limping as I walked.
My shoes were too small.

They'd created ingrown nails
on each of my big toes, and
I could feel when I stepped on a piece of gravel
just perfectly.
The shoes were so small that even the
slightest pressure like stepping on gravel,
caused more irritation and pain.
They had become infected a month ago:
red, swollen, and oozing milky,
green puss.

I had already told Father
I needed new shoes,
and they were purchased.

However, he had taken them back from me
the very next day, as a
form of punishment.
Throwing them at me
and hitting me with them,
as he took the desperately needed
new sneakers.
I was denied the basic necessity of
proper footwear.

"These are *my* shoes!"
he yelled at me.

He forced me back into my old shoes,
which were two sizes too small.

I reminded him about my toes as well,

repeatedly,
but he told me they would be alright.

I made it into the house after my rather painful
quarter of a mile walk,
sat on my bed,
and kicked my shoes off with a sigh of relief.

My socks were stained with
hardened blood and puss
from the infections.
I slowly pulled them off,
wincing as I unstuck each sock from the
painful sores.

At this point,
I didn't know what to do.
I did know, I'd had enough.

Even though the housekeeper
did the family's laundry weekly,
I didn't have enough clothes to
make it through the week
like the rest of my family did.
That night I was in the laundry room
washing my clothes and
I called to Father,
telling him I thought I really needed
to see a doctor about my feet.
They really hurt now.

Father began telling me
he thought my toes would be fine.

Once he finished the first sentence,
I cut him off,
"The *fucking* doctor knows more than you!"

"Watch your mouth!" he replied sternly.
"No!" I yelled back.

Hearing the bar stool slide,
I looked up my from laundry
just in time to see my belligerent,
red faced dad barreling toward me.

He grabbed me by the throat and
slammed me against the bathroom door.
He sprayed spit in my face as he yelled
while holding me against the door,
his grip getting tighter and tighter.

I was only fifteen and
struggled against the old farmer's grip,
only able to get a hold of his thumb.
I pulled back with all my might, which
made him release me,
but then he grabbed my arm,
swung me away from the door,
and threw me right back against it,
reaffirming a grasp
on my throat.

My sister Rachel, could hear my choked words as
I tried to tell Father to let go of me.
"He's gonna kill him!"
I heard her scream to mom.
"He's not gonna kill him," Mom replied.

My mom's resolve against my father
on my behalf,
dwindled over the years.
Not that her love for me was less,
she just had her own battles with him.

With one final squeeze, tighter than the rest
and using his nails, he finally let go of me.

I immediately ran to the office
across the house to call the police

while Father walked to his bedroom.
I showed the police the bruising scratches
on my neck,
they asked me whether I wanted
my father to be taken to jail
that night or not.
In my frazzled state, I replied to the officers,
telling them I didn't know
if I wanted him taken.

I had empathy for my father.
I knew he had a lot to lose.
Not only did he have the
ranch we lived on to look after,
he had a team of employees under him
who relied on him for paychecks.
If my father went away, it affected a lot of people.
And despite the years of abuse
he was still my dad.

The police then went into Father's bedroom
and spoke to him.

They did not end up taking my dad that night,
and things did slightly improve at home.
But not in a way you would hope.

Father couldn't believe I would
file a police report on him.

He thought of it as a form of betrayal.

How *dare* I get outsiders
involved in our family business!

For the foreseeable future,
I was to stay in my room if I
wasn't at school.

For meals,

Father slid quesadillas
under my door, or
he would leave food by the door,
knock, and then run away.
I could hear the change of
pace in his footsteps—
long, slow strides to the door,
short, quick steps away, to avoid me.

Misplaced

I sat on the edge of my bed,
deep in thought.
I was holding a relatively cheap
gas station knife in my hand
and staring at the veins on my wrist.

I could never please Father,
and he treated me poorly
because of it.
I thought of myself as a nuisance
to Mom and Rachel.
No one ever seemed happy with me.

And most of all,
Father would never let me go
live with Mother.

I wasn't a fish out of water with her.

My current situation,
in my young mind,
seemed sempiternal.

I contemplated whether the
physical pain of the knife
would be worth obtaining
the perpetual antidote.

Part 11

I woke, startled and dazed
from the sudden flood of light.
I opened my eyes to see two large men
entering my room,
followed by Father.

"These guys are going to take you to school,"
he announced sternly.

One of the men threw the shirt and pants
I had been wearing the day prior at me.

As I hesitantly put my clothes on,
I kept a wary eye on the men
and said nothing.

I had many questions as to what was going on,
but I played along and did as I was told,
saying nothing
to avoid a conflict.
I knew I couldn't win.

Before they escorted me out to their SUV,
they gave me flip-flops,
which I found odd.
I never wore flip-flops.

Once I was in the vehicle,
I could see Father and the strange men
talking outside.

I need to get out of here,
I thought to myself.

I tried the door handle,
but was immediately defeated by
child safety locks.
I thought about breaking the windows,
but I wasn't willing to accept the
potential consequences.

After a moment,
the men entered the vehicle
and we began our drive.

"What's happening?"
I asked them.
"You're going to a boarding school in New York,"
one of them answered.
"Called the Academy at Ivy Ridge.
It's a school in upstate New York for struggling youth,
like yourself."

Hearing that,
I didn't think much.

I was struggling in school,
the only time I had succeeded at
school, was in Reno with Mother,
away from Father.
So, maybe this would be a good thing.
But I still needed to call Mother

and my girlfriend
to let them know what was going on.

"You'll get phone calls at the school,"
one of the men replied when I asked.

I was excited and curious at the same time,
thinking about my new school.
I wasn't going to have
Father breathing down my neck,
and maybe I would actually have help.

They tuned the radio to 96.7 FM at my request,
and we continued our drive to the airport;
"Vermillion" by Slipknot on the radio.

Academy At Ivy Ridge
STUDENT EDUCATION PLAN

Colin Patrick Buckley   State: CA
Student Name

Pride   Date: 20-Dec-04
Family Name

Student Courses	Credit Earned	Grade	Credit Needed	Student Courses	Credit Earned	Grade	Credit Needed
HS				Academy at Ivy Ridge			
9th Grade				10th Grade			
N General PE	0.50	B		English 10			1.00
English 1	0.50	B		Geometry			1.00
Skills Ac Suc 1-2	0.50	D		Earth Science			1.00
Phy Science	0.00	F		Civics			0.50
Wrld Geo/Religions	0.00	F		Spanish 1			1.00
Alg Essen 1	0.50	C-		Study Skills	0.50	90	
Out of State				PE Fitness			0.50
9th Grade				11th grade			
English 2	0.50	A-		English 11			
Reading Renaissanc	0.50	A-		Algebra II			1.00
Woodwkg 1	0.50	B-		Chemistry			1.00
Physical Sci 2	0.50	D		US History			1.00
World Geog 2	0.50	C		12th Grade			1.00
Algebra Crs 1B	0.50	C-		English 12			
HS				US Gov't/Economics			1.00
10th Grade				Bus. Pers. Finance			1.00
English 3-4	0.00	F		Art Elective			1.00
Spanish 1	0.00	F		Health			0.50
Biology	0.00	D-		PE Fitness			1.00
World Hist	0.00	F		Elective			2.00
St Ag Wel 1H	0.00	F		Elective			2.00
Alg Essen 2	0.00	F		Elective			1.00

Graduation Requirements	General	College
English	4	4
Math	3	3
Science	3	3
Social Studies	4	4
Art	1	1
Physical Education	1	1
Health	0.5	0.5
Vocational	1	1
Computer	0.5	0.5
Electives	6	4
Foreign Language	-	2
Total Credits	24	24

Credits Earned 5.50
Credits Needed 18.50

Total Credits 24.00

Students GPA 2.64

Misplaced

***

All I needed
was a little bit of freedom,
and
to be treated
like I was human.

***

It was cold.
My shirt was thin and
it wasn't doing much.

That's odd,
I thought to myself.
Why are there grates on the windows?
"Good luck getting through those doors
in case you're thinking about it.
They're magnetized,"
the man with the clipboard informed me.

They had me follow them into a room
where they had me strip down and
searched through my things.

After they were done,
they had me dress in a pair of sweats my
parents had apparently packed for me and
walked with me to a computer room.

"This is your family,
and this is your Hope Buddy,"
the man said while gesturing to
another student.

Just then,
a student on the other side of the room
began yelling and kicked his chair over.

"Don't worry.
He's flipping out.
It happens sometimes."
my buddy said,
as the student was picked up and
slammed to the floor by three staff members.
I didn't think much about what I saw,
I received similar consequences at home.

This was normal to me.

Shortly after,
we lined up and boarded a bus.
The ride was only a couple of minutes
from the schoolhouse to the barracks.

"You have to sleep here
in case you attempt suicide,"
stated the dorm dad.

Suicide? At "school?"
I learned quickly that this
wasn't the school I was hoping for.

There was an old musty mattress
centered in the hallway of the barracks
at the foot of the night guard.

"Here's a sheet," he said,
tossing it to me.

"Don't worry about the lights.
They're always on.
Now go to sleep."

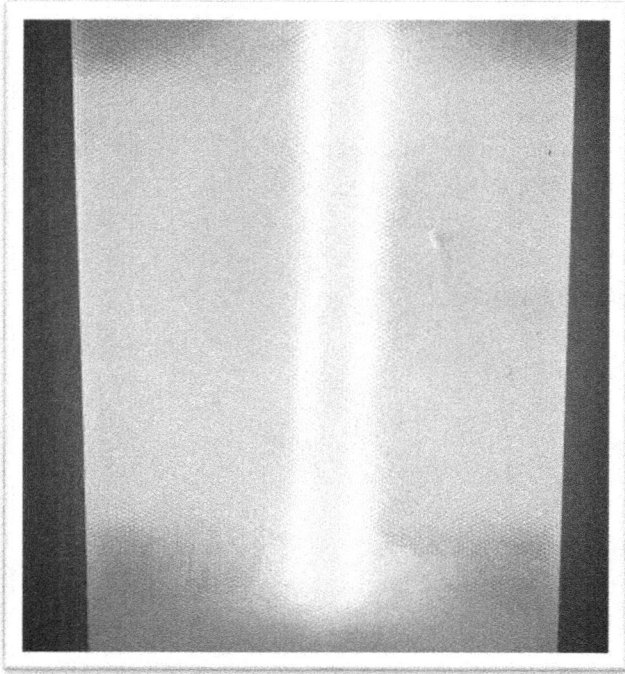

***

The chaos never relented,
and I witnessed levels of
violence daily.
At least once a day a student would "flip out"
and be, what they called, "restrained."
They would pick the kids up and slam them
to the tile floors.
Any injury that the student acquired in the process
would be annotated, and
the blame would be placed on the student.

During the day we were expected to
work on school work.
I was already behind,
and I had no one to help me.
No one who knew what they were doing,
anyway.

I was stuck.

We had "group" to talk about our feelings
once a day.
As if those pieces of shit
cared about the kids' feelings.

I was alright;
surviving and
going through the motions.

A ghost.

***

We were sitting in the computer lab and
mail was being handed out.
I didn't have my hopes up about getting
any mail because
I couldn't even picture my dad sitting down
to take the time to write me a letter.

"Colin, here you go."
I was startled when I heard my name.
I couldn't believe it.
I looked up and took the letter from our dorm dad,
and eagerly tore it open and began to read.

As I did, tears of sadness and hopelessness
welled in my eyes.

It was what they called a "commitment letter."

My Hope Buddy heard me sniffle and looked over.

"We all get those. Don't worry about it. You could
be here longer, or you could be here shorter.
They don't really mean anything,"
he whispered under his breath to me.

"I just don't want to flip out," I whispered back.

"What are you talking about? You're good, man.
"No one's provoking you," he said to me.

I said nothing in reply.
I don't think he understood what I
meant by my statement.

I knew if I had to live in these conditions, and
under this much structure,
it was only a matter of time before I was restrained.
I was eventually going to lose my cool and

end up like one of the kids I saw every day,
getting slammed by multiple grown men.

It looked like it hurt, and I was scared.

They would kneel on the kids' necks, backs,
arms, and legs.
I was only 115-120 pounds.
I knew it was only a matter of time because
I didn't like seeing it happen and
I knew one day it was going to be
one of my friends, and
I would flip out too because of it.
I could maintain my composure
until it came to people I cared for.
In only a few days,
I started to feel bonded
to the other kids in my "family."

Colin Buckley   DOE   11/9/04

November 13, 2004

Dear Colin;

We hope that you are adjusting well to your new school. I bet you look handsome in your new uniform! Just a quick note to let you know that we are committed to you staying at Ivy Ridge for a year or until your graduation. We know that this school is going to help you get the skills that you are going to need to have a productive life. They will help you with your manners, relationships with family and other people, education and social skills.

Colin, we would really like for you to try really hard to follow directions, be smart, make some good friends. This school will offer you the building blocks of life, so please learn from them. So, try hard because this is your new lease on life and please remember that we love you and that is why we sent you to Ivy Ridge.

Dad

♡ mom

***

Most of the time, the food was bad,
spoiled, and/or plain.
I'll admit there were a few dishes they
served that were decent,
or they were the best of the worst.
The chicken cordon bleu was ok.

I learned to drink my juice last and
treat it like a dessert.
I always hoped
the blue kind was left
by the time I got to the dispenser.

But most of the time, the
dark purple kind was the only one left,
and it made my mouth itch
because I was allergic to something in it,
so I was left with water—
not to be filled above the line on our cups.

When we were served oatmeal,
it was plain oatmeal in a bowl.

Sometimes if we were lucky and
our family ate first,
we would get the bowls
topped with a teaspoon of
brown sugar.

If it was a lucky day,
I would eat around the ball
of sugar,
and save that for last
and then chase it with
my juice.

***

Father had me taken in November,
just before my sixteenth birthday.
I had already missed that,
so I wondered
how they celebrated Christmas
at this "school."

Maybe we'll get to watch a movie.
Maybe we'll get cake,
I thought to myself.

Even though my thoughts
remained somewhat optimistic,
I knew better than to get my hopes up.
Especially in a place like this.

I was learning quickly.

This place had a way of taking even the
slightest amount of happiness
and smashing it like an insect.

How is the shower water
this cold already?
I thought to myself.

Jesus Christ,
He's jerking off, and
my shower is the one with the drain.

***

I could hear another student
getting beaten by his bunk leader:
thuds and the occasional slap.

A whispered "Owe!"
and
"Shut up!"
could be heard from across the hall.
The student being beaten was
much smaller than his bunk leader.

This happened regularly;
at least every other night.

The night watch was at the end of the hallway,
out of earshot of the commotion.
Not only was he too far away,
students often yelled obscenities
whenever it became too quiet
in an attempt to be funny;
it was never really quiet at bedtime.

I thought what was happening was wrong,
but I didn't dare interfere,
and neither did the others.

No one wanted the label of "snitch."

Later in life,
I reconnected with a friend
from this "school,"
and learned the student in the room,
across the hall
was raped and no one ever stopped it
or said a word.

This happened in a room that slept four.

***

We were made to participate in seminars.
There was a total of seven we had to complete
in order to progress in the school's program.

I made it through the orientation seminar—
everyone does.

Discovery wasn't as easy to pass
as orientation was.
Everyone had to participate.

I said nothing and watched.

They would give the children assignments,
but each one had a twist.
If the instructions called for a full page of writing,
that's what they meant.
We were to write in the header space
and past the margin lines.
They would add odd requests
like, adding a diamond in specific
places on the page.
If you didn't follow the instructions given,
you failed,
having to leave and then
repeat the seminar at a later date, and
they were held monthly.

> program   to   wor
> rules   but   that
> the   program   diffe
> prison. That   is
> ht   now. Is   that
> what   I   did
> we   beat   me,   wh
> also   should
> my   biologica
> she   gave   me   a
> said   that. He   si
> that   I   want   to
> lad   killed   himself   in
> note   attached   to him,
> that   I   was   ad
> bring   out   was
> that   I   wanted   t
> sted   me   died   when

I couldn't make it through this one
being quiet.

So, I failed.
When we failed these seminars,
the blame fell on the kids.
The ones in charge would tell the children they were
"choosing out"
instead of being kicked out.

I chose out of the seminar
because I was too quiet,
and that was my choice.

They weren't wrong.
I had no interest in
completing these seminars.
I thought they were culty and
weird.

So I remained in the back,
attempting to remain unnoticed,

but it didn't work.

I was caught being quiet.
They made me stand up in front of everyone
to explain myself.
"This isn't for me,"
I stated.

I feared stating my
actual opinion:
this was crazy, ludicrous,
and I didn't want any part of it.

They were trying to brainwash us.

I was escorted out of the room,
but they didn't bring me back to class.
Instead, I was taken to what they called
Intervention.

Intervention was a small,
roughly ten by ten, room,
where the "problem students" were to sit and
stare at the wall.

Sometimes students would get rowdy,
fight,

and cause problems for the
dorm parent in charge that day.
Who could blame them, though?
This place was maddening.

When that happened,
the dorm dad in charge would
open up the windows,
using the weather to his advantage.

It was wintertime in upstate New York,
which meant it was always
around -10 to 20°F outside.
With the room being concrete and small,
the temperature would drop instantly—
freezing the kids.

The dorm dad would stand outside of the room
until he thought the kids had enough of the
frigid temperatures.

Three times I "chose out" of the seminar,
and was placed in this room.
Sometimes I was alone, and
other times there were a
couple of other students with me.
I was being punished for not
making it through their seminars and
"working my program."

***

I sat in the computer lab,
running my fingers over the
fresh new little tattoo
I had given myself.
It was an arrow in the stars to
symbolize Sagittarius.

When we wanted to tattoo ourselves,
we used a gel pen and the little clothes pins
that came in our uniform clothes.

By this time, I had given up because
progression seemed impossible.
I had taken the same test
over and over again for school,
and the program required
mechanical perfection for everything,
which I did not possess at the time.
And no one cared to help us.

As I sat there looking at my arm,
a dorm dad came up behind me and
grabbed my wrist.
"What is that?" he asked,
already knowing the answer.

He maintained a grip on my arm and
started walking toward the front of the lab,
dragging me from my seat.

"Hey bro, you got a 408 over here,"
he said to our family's dorm dad.

When we received a consequence,
we received a little half sheet
piece of paper to fill out.
If we filled it out,
our consequence was

just the normal sentence.
If we made the staff fill it out,
our consequence doubled.

"Staff it," I said when the dorm dad
as he tried to hand me the consequence.

I received a 408: tattooing/piercing/disfiguring.
Consequence: Eight hours in study hall and
complete loss of points.

Since a category four consequence
took all our points from us and
I had been stuck in the same spot on my
schoolwork for a couple months now,
I didn't care about staying in
study hall for an extra day.

My progress in the program and
with my schoolwork was
stagnant anyway.

The next day, after breakfast,
we lined up for meds and
I was called up by the nurse.
I never took any medication, so
I wondered why I was being called.
As I got up to the window,
she reached over the counter and
grabbed my wrist,
pulling my arm over the counter toward her.

"Your dad gave us permission to
remove layers of skin if we need to,
to get this off," she said to me.

That sounds like him, I thought to myself.
Then she opened a small package and
started scrubbing my tattoo with a little, abrasive,
medicated towelette.

I had no idea what it was,
but it hurt.

She scrubbed until the
scabbing all came off and
my arm started to bleed.
She finally stopped,
looked at it, and said,

"Ya, that's not coming off.
Are you happy with that?"

I didn't respond to her.
I just pulled my sleeve back down and
walked away from the counter to
fall back in line.
I still had the other half of my
study hall sentence to carry out.

From: c@academyivyridge.com]
Sent: Monday, January 10, 2005 11:43 AM
To:
Subject: Conference Call Results

A conference call was done , on Monday, January 10, 2005 at 11:00 am in the office of ▓▓▓ with ▓▓▓ and Kim Buckley regarding their son, Colin Buckley of the Pride Family. Entry date November 9, 2004. Those in attendance were ▓▓▓

Topics discussed were:
   Academics: Alton addressed what subjects Colin is currently in and how much work he is taking. However, Colin continues to not pass tests. We spoke about how when his behavior comes into line more his academics will follow also. Alton said he will be looking into following Colin more closely on his tests to assist him in areas that may need more assistance in.

   Behavior: ▓▓▓ discussed what has happening with Colin regarding what kind of consequences he is receiving. Most of them are Category 1's at this time. However, some bad attitude will appear at times and he earns more severe consequences. Colin did a tattoo with a staple and ink from a pen. Parents want the school to have it removed by brushing with a brush and soap. ▓▓▓ stated we would look into having it removed by the medical staff and get back to them.

Alton never came to my aid.

115

***

I had gotten to this supposed
"school" in the wintertime,
and now it was almost spring.
It was a locked down facility,
meaning I had only been
outside three times in the past
four months.

Maybe once a month we would get outside time,
which consisted of walking around the courtyard
in a single file line around a gazebo.

I could see the sunshine outside,
and feel it every so often as
I passed by the windows while we walked
in line from point A to point B.

One day, I was looking down and noticed
one of the freckles on my arm that was normally
bigger and browner than the rest
was more orangish.

It was fading because of the lack of sunshine.
That's it! I thought to myself.

As much of an asshole I thought Father was,
I knew if there was one thing he didn't agree with, it was
kids staying inside.

He was a farmer and thought
kids should always be outside
doing something productive.

So I wrote to him saying
I would like to go outside more often.

The school probably wouldn't deny
my claim, or hold my letter back

because I actually said I had been outside
in it, just not as often as I liked.
It was also pretty open about outside activities
being an upper-level privilege—
in the school students were given levels
based on a point system.
A system designed for failure.
Feet not flat on the floor,
minus five points.
Burping, minus five points.
Arms not by your side,
minus five points.
The average time it took for a student to
complete the program was two years.
Despite the initial commitment of
one year.

I was hoping the letter would reach him,
but I did have my doubts.

My goal wasn't to get home.
I knew that was probably far-fetched because
I had been sent away already.
My goal was to be sent to another school.

I just hoped the next one was a
normal boarding school.

***

Another student and I were horsing around,
snapping each other with our sweater vests.

One of the dorm dads passed by the room
and made a subtle comment,
telling us to knock it off.

Us being teenage boys, we
continued our horseplay,
disregarding the dorm dad's order.

Within a couple of seconds,
another dorm dad reached in and
grabbed two fistfuls of my shirt:
one hand on my chest,
and the other on my back.

He heaved me out of the room and
slammed me into the concrete wall in the hallway,
causing me to hit my eyebrow.

I jammed my hand in my pocket for the face razor
I had snapped in half to create a weapon.
I never planned to use it,
but I had seen enough of what goes on
in this place
to know I'd rather have a weapon
than not.

Holding my cheap homemade blade in my hand,
I stood still,
contemplating whether to go for the man's face
or neck.

Would juvie be better than here?
I wondered as the dorm dad
projected saliva with his screams
inches from my face.

Once he was done yelling,
he released me and
I ran to the bathroom.

I punched the walls several times
and screamed as hard as I could
out of anger and frustration.

I was helpless.
There was no escape.
I felt like a crazed, caged animal.

The dorm dad followed me,
attempting to speak,
but I didn't want to hear it.

What happened was wrong.

He didn't deserve to be heard by me.

"Get the fuck away from me!"
I demanded and walked to the
other side of the bathroom.

After that, he walked out of the bathroom,
smirking.

I hated it there.
I wanted out.

I didn't deserve to be in this place.

All I ever wanted was to live with my mother,
where I was loved and happy.
Why was that not possible for me?
Why was love and happiness so unreachable for me?

Instead, it seemed to get further and further
away.

Father sent me away for being unruly,
for arguing with him and
battling with him over my happiness.

Now I was stuck in a place with
no contact with the outside world.
I couldn't talk to my mother,
brothers, or my girlfriend—
no one.

I was only allowed to send
one filtered letter a week to Father—
no one else.

Trapped and forced into survival mode
even more than I was before.

Restrained

INCIDENT REPORT FORM

STUDENT: Colin Buckley   DATE: 2/24/05

TIME: 9:15 pm   DORM PARENT SUPERVISOR: ███████

PARENT COORDINATOR: _____   FAMILY REP: Ta███

DETAILS: Around 9ᵗʰ pm Pride family was instructed to line up for night prep. I observed the Pride family Continually fooling around and not following their dorm dad, ██████ instructions. I walked down to assist Mr. Jarod and saw Colin Buckley wipping another student, Justin ████ with a Sweater vest inside their dorm room. I yelled at Colin to stop and he continued laughing and attempting to whip Justin one last time. I told Justin to get in line and told Colin to do the same. Colin Continued horseplaying with Justin ████ so I Madt restrained him to put him in the hallway, while Madt restraining Colin Buckley he Continued to struggle and threw his body around causing his own head to hit the wall. He then stopped struggling so I released the Madt restraint hold and asked him to calm down. Colin Buckley remained calm in line but while in the bathroom prepping Continued to scream and continue to be out of control. The Pride family calmed him down and spoke with him until shutdown.

Was an appropriate action taken? Yes   Explain: Colin was whipping another student and was stopped before he hurt that student.

Was excessive force used? No   If yes, explain: _____

X ███████
X _____
PRINT WRITER'S NAME

X ████
X John ████
PRINT WITNESS'S NAME

121

***

I was attempting to do my schoolwork
when I heard my name called.
I looked up and saw it was the dorm dad
I'd had a confrontation with the night before.

Confused,
I stood from my seat and went with him.

I didn't have a choice.
I didn't want to go,
but if I didn't comply
they would have pulled me from my chair.
If I resisted or struggled,
I would have been restrained and dragged
to study hall.

As we made our way down the hallway,
we were silent.
I didn't want to talk to him after
last night's event.

We made a sharp right and
headed through the door to the courtyard;
right in the middle stood the gazebo.

"I want you to shovel the snow from
one side of the gazebo to the other."
the dorm dad instructed me.

I happily complied.
It was anywhere from 10 to 20°F outside.
He wanted to play games and
I was no stranger to shovel work. I grew up on a farm.
I knew he would get cold a lot faster than I would
because I was working.

I moved a couple shovelfuls of snow,
and then took off my blazer,

dress shirt, and tie,
leaving only my T-shirt

Scoop after scoop, I moved the snow.
The chilly weather was no problem,
and it felt good on my swollen eyebrow.

After a while
the dorm dad caved in,
needing to go inside to get out of the cold.

Being alone at the school was forbidden
unless you were level four or higher,
so, I had to go in with him.

I had no clue as to why the dorm dad was
attempting to antagonize me.
The only thing I could think of
was that he didn't like the way I had reacted to his
attack the night before.

I believe he knew he was wrong,
but he needed to be confident in his actions
to maintain a level of authority
because we students couldn't be right.

Gazebo

***

I sat looking out of the window
(Cat 1—off task, minus five points)
at the snow on the ground because
I couldn't get past a particular section
in my science work…still.

I had requested help, but no one came.
There was only one actual teacher
who came around to the computer lab
to "help" students.

It seemed like the questions on the test
didn't even pertain to the chapter I read.

How would I convince a teacher of that?

I heard my name called and
when I looked up to see who it was,
I let out a breath of annoyance.

It was the same dorm dad
who had made me shovel snow
the day before.
What could he possibly want this time?

He called another student to come with us and
we left the computer lab.

That was a bit of a relief
because I always felt a little safer having
someone with me when I was
with the staff in this place.

He took us to the bathroom and
handed us each a toothbrush.
"Get to it! Scrub the floor!"
he ordered us.

Without saying anything,
we both got down and began
meticulously cleaning the bathroom floor.

I sat on my hands and knees,
scrubbing, and
wondered how long he was
going to have us there,
but said nothing.
He was the one who had
wrongfully attacked me a
couple of days ago.
Why was he trying to provoke me?
What did I ever do to this guy?
I didn't get it.

All I knew was that I couldn't let this place win.
So I'd go through the motions,
picking and choosing my battles.

If I had to wait it out here
in this "school" until I was eighteen,
so be it.

***

I shot a three pointer and
made it with a clean swish.

I wasn't very good at basketball,
but I could shoot pretty consistently.
Besides, the hour of gym time
was the most exercise we received
in the "school."

The rest of the time we were
sitting at a computer,
in a room with windows
we weren't allowed to look out of,
or
walking in a single file line somewhere.

Right after I made the shot, the
dorm dad I disliked the most
walked into the gym.

He immediately called our family to
line up against the wall and ordered us
to start wall squats.
He would say up, and we would come up and
when he said down, we were to go down.

"Up, down, up, down, up, down, up, down!"
he screamed.
We would get a rhythm going and then
he would stop.
Some kids would come up
when he stopped on "down" and the
same thing would happen when he stopped
on "up."

Every time students would mess up by
anticipating his command,
he would make us start over.

We didn't even know what our
goal number was
because he never told us.
We just started exercising.

Finally, a student snapped.

He started screaming and
walked toward the dorm dad.
As soon as he was within reach,
the dorm dad picked him up and
slammed him to the floor.

That's when I lost it.

I broke from the wall and yelled,
"Fuck you! You provoked him!" And then,
I walked to the door and
punched it as hard as I could.
A group of kids from my family
surrounded me,
trying to calm me before it escalated and
I ended up getting slammed, too.

I turned around,
opened the door, and
walked out into the hallway.
I only made it a couple of steps before
I heard footsteps racing up behind me.

Normally, when we ran out into the
hall by ourselves, we were tackled.
But I turned around to look at who it was,
and it was a different dorm dad.

Lucky for me,
one of the more mild tempered ones.

"Where are you going?" he asked me.

"Study hall," I answered.

At this time,
I would rather be there than
be stuck with an angry, red-faced dorm dad
who was on a power trip.

"You're not allowed to be alone,"
he said as he trotted to catch up to me.
"Why not? It's not like I can fucking walk outside,"
I answered smartly.

He didn't say anything to that.
Instead, he walked beside me to study hall.

Some dorm dads were better than others.
Some weren't as hostile and
actually, seemed to care for us.
It was either that,
or they were just the best of the worst.

But this one seemed alright.

From: ███████ s [malesuper1@academyivyridge com]
Sent: Saturday March 12, 2005 10:58 PM
To:

Subject: incident

Colin Buckley of the pride family punched the wall in the gym because he was frustrated with his dorm parent.
Medical staff checked him over.

No, they didn't.

***

"Yo, let's go!"
I looked up from my computer and
saw our dorm dad looking at me.

I closed out my screen on the computer and
got up to follow him.

"Your dad's here.
You're going home," he said
as we got out into the hallway.

"My dad!?" I exclaimed.
I was shocked and surprised.
It didn't seem like something my
dad would do.
If anything, he would send for me,
not come to get me himself.

We got to my room and I
quickly gathered my things.
As we made our way back toward the
front of the school,
I squinted down the hallway to make out
who was standing by the front door, and
my heart sunk.

It was not my father.

There was a shorter, stockier man
with white hair and glasses.
Next to him,
stood a taller man who obviously never missed
a day in the gym.
He wore black combat boots,
BDU pants,
an olive green T-shirt,
and kept his hair in a high fade.

"That's not my dad." I stated to the dorm dad.

"Oh," he said.
"That means they're transporters."

Great, I thought to myself.
That means I'm going to another "school."
I wonder which one Father chose this time.

By this time, I had heard of other
facilities like the one I was in.
The more infamous ones talked about
amongst the students were in
Utah, Jamaica, Mississippi, and
Baja, California.

Supposedly, they were all worse than
where I was currently, which meant
the letter I wrote to Father
some time ago,
asking to go outside, had made it to him.
Instead of just bringing me home or
sending me to a normal boarding school
after four months,
he chose to transfer me to another facility;
a military based one.

When we reached the two men,
I shook hands with them and winced.
The bigger guy asked me what was wrong and
I revealed my bruised knuckles I had acquired
during the dorm dad's game he played with us
a couple of days prior.
"Well, that's not good," the man said after
I explained the situation.

After some brief small talk,
we walked outside and got into a car.

We turned onto the highway and headed south

132

to Lucedale, MS.
Eagle Point Christian Academy.

From: @academyivyridge.com]
Sent: Tuesday, February 22, 2005 12:20 PM
To:
Subject: FW: collin buckly-   (dad)

-----Original Message-----
From: @helpmyteen.com]
Sent: Tuesday, February 22, 2005 12:05 PM
To:
Cc:
Subject: collin buckly-   (dad)

dad is calling me

Dad has given ivy a try- what is up with there

the consequences are not changing the kid.

Says that the kid never goes outside

kid is not passing school

he has been outside 3 time in 4 months

he is sitting there playing on the computer

he feels he is just getting lip service- but nothing is changing- dad feels he is wasting money- not getting any better

dad feels that collin is just a kid on the books and not getting the attention he needs

dad says the kid is difficult

i am asking that he contact

Misplaced

From: [redacted]2@academyivyridge.com]
Sent: Tuesday, March 15, 2005 8:25 PM
To:

Subject: EXIT

[redacted] and Colin Buckley exited the school today. They were picked up by escorts and brought to Eagle Point Academy.

Part 12

We pulled off the road and onto a
concrete driveway.
To our left there was a chain-link fence with
dividers in it,
and to the right there was a church.
The trees were thick all around.

We made a left and
parked in front of a wooden building.
Behind us and to the right
was an empty grass field.

Maybe they actually let us do sports here.
I stupidly thought to myself.

Another student I recognized from
my last facility was there in the building.
He told me this was a Marine based disciplinary
boot camp,
and warned me to not fuck around—
they didn't play there.

Within the fence, there were three buildings.
One was a two story, and
housed Charley company,
Bravo company, and Eval cadets.
Charley and Eval were on top.
The building in the middle was the school building,
and the third building housed Alpha
company cadets.

All living spaces were an open bay
with the bathrooms located at the end.

I was escorted to the top story of the
furthest building
and ordered to sit on the floor near the front desk,
which was located in front of the door.

The other students had already eaten their dinner.
So, the drill instructor sent a couple of students to get me a
tray from the chow hall.

As I waited for my food,
I glanced around at the other students.
They all had their heads shaved and looked fit.
They wore BDU pants tucked into black boots and yellow T-shirts.
They all stood perfectly still,
facing inward toward the middle of the bay
at the end of their assigned bunks.
Their arms sat at their sides as the
drill instructor paced back and forth,
giving them instruction.

"Yes, sir!" they replied in unison
whenever the DI paused.

When the cadets returned with my food,
I opened my tray and there was nothing but
beans and lettuce.

I knew this place was supposedly worse than

the last facility I was in,
but I didn't think it was going to be this bad.

The only thing I could think to do was
mix the salad and beans together to hopefully
give the plain lettuce some flavor.

Hopefully, the food isn't this bad all the time,
I thought to myself as I ate.
It was nearing lights out
by the time I finished my chow,
so they dragged a mattress over and
threw it in the middle of the bay floor.

Just like my last facility,
for the first night I was on suicide watch,
with nothing but a bed sheet to keep me warm
on a filthy mattress.
Only this time I had to sleep in the
middle of an open bay with
other students all around me.

As the other students got ready for bed,
they spoke quietly
and I caught their glances.

I felt vulnerable,
laying there with my head
underneath the sheet, trying to sleep.

This place seemed worse and
all I had done was write to Father,
complaining that the last place I was in
never let us go outside.

Now I was stuck in a
whole different kind of hell.

I just wanted out of these "schools."
I wanted to be happy and free,

but it seemed so far out of reach.

I wondered what my mother and brothers were doing,
and if they knew where I was.
I was never given a chance to talk to them
before my father had me taken to my last "school,"
four months earlier.

Lucky for me,
my head was covered,
so the other students couldn't
see the tears rolling from my eyes.

***

I was placed in the evaluation platoon,
where I learned new terminology and
facing movements.
I had to learn to march and
a whole new way of speaking.
We had to ask permission to speak,
and speak in third person.

If we needed to use the bathroom,
we would sound off with:
"Sir, this cadet requests permission
to speak, sir."
"Speak!" the drill instructor would say.
"Sir, this cadet requests permission to make
a head call, sir!"

Sometimes they wouldn't let us go, and
when they did allow us to use the head,
they only gave us two minutes.

We had the same time constraints
when it came to showers as well.
We were taught to
"Hit the hot spots and get out."
Meaning our head, arm pits, private areas, and feet.

The drill instructors were merciless.
They would have us doing pushups unceasingly.

DI: "Up!"
Us: "One, sir!"
DI: "Down!"
DI: "Up!"
Us: "Two, sir!"
DI: "Down!"
As they paced up and down the bay.

Sometimes they would have us going so long,

I would lose count.
When I would try to hear the number the
other cadets were saying,
I wouldn't be able to make it out
because we were all too
impoverished to sound off coherently.

When the drill instructors would have us do an
excessive amount in one sitting,
our form would diminish, and our chests would
hit the wood floor with a loud thud
whenever they said, "Down."

It was a split second of relief to
lay on the floor
before they said "Up" again.

It didn't matter if they had us do
a thousand pushups the day before
and we couldn't physically lift our arms anymore.
They would still have us get down and do them
whenever a cadet did something he
wasn't supposed to:

mass punishment.

Everyone was responsible for everyone.
If one person screwed up,
we all had to pay the price.

One time in particular, they had us do
over three hundred pushups consecutively
before they let us go to bed.
Most of the time they only had us go into the
200's.

These exercise sessions were called "getting smoked."
The drill instructors would "smoke" us.

It was exhausting and painful.

I couldn't bend my arms to
touch my shoulders.

Pushups weren't their only torture method.
There was enough room between each of the buildings
for us to bear crawl and crab walk
until our hands were raw from the dirt.
Or they would simply march us out the gate to the
field that sat on the other side of the driveway,
and smoke us there.

Another one of their favorites was having us
duck walk in a line while we
held onto the shoulders of the person in front of us.
Holding onto each other
made it more difficult because it
forced us to push and pull on each other to
maintain our balance and move in unison.

The drill instructors who worked at the facility,
were mostly Marine Corps veterans,
and knew exactly how to break us off.
Sometimes, we would come back
to the barracks after
forced church service or chow,
to find our bay destroyed.
Bed sheets tossed everywhere,
mattresses flipped, and
bathroom, aka "the head," destroyed.
Everything was thrashed.

They would call us to attention and
give us three minutes to clean it up,
and if we failed,
we would get smoked.
Then they would give us a
shorter amount of time to finish cleaning,
and if we failed,
they would smoke us again.

Sometimes, it seemed like the
punishment never relented.

It would continue until every last
hospital corner was folded on every bed or "rack,"
and each rack had two hand-widths of
white bed sheet showing at the head of it.
If cadets refused to comply, they would be
dragged into the bathroom by the
drill instructors and "corrected."

There were no cameras in the bathrooms.

School was done in little booklets,
and we only worked on them for a
couple of hours a day.

It was a break we
received during the day from the
relentless physical exertion
forced upon us.

Even though all of this was
my new reality,
to me, Eagle Point was actually
better than Ivy Ridge.
There were no seminars,
our uniforms weren't bad,
and I was becoming a machine,
physically and mentally.

Every once in a while, the DIs would have us
gather around to sit and talk to us.
Even though we had these sit downs and
were allowed to "speak freely,"
we didn't dare complain.
The little gathering was another
break from being smoked.

We were like abused dogs
trying to keep our masters happy
by talking about what they wanted,
and conversing with them as if
we looked up to them.

During one of these sit downs,
one of the dis went as far as to
tell us about the time he spent in the
red-light district while he was
stationed overseas in the Marine Corps.

He told us how he went into one of the
"whore houses" and had a woman
sit in a swing that hung from the ceiling,
and spin on his dick.

During another one of these gatherings,
one of the cadets asked if the
Marine Corps was this difficult.

"Is the real Marines this hard, sir?"
the boy asked.

"You guys get it worse than Paris Island," he replied.

***

It had almost been about seven months since
Father and I fought about me going
to the doctor for my feet.

When I was at Ivy Ridge,
I did tell them about the infection in my toes,
but nothing ever came of it.
I had lived with the pain of the
infection so long that I didn't press the issue,
I was used to it.

But this facility was different.
All the running around and the
pushups aggravated the infection,
and the pain of the ingrown toenails
became excruciating.

To my surprise,
the school actually made me a
doctor's appointment.

Within a couple of days of telling them,
I was called out of my company and
jumped into a car with another student
who had an off-campus appointment too.

After the operation,
I remained silent
in the back seat of the car as we
drove back to the campus.

The rock station was on and
tears had welled in my eyes
hearing the music.
I could feel it in my chest and throat
as I held back my emotion.
It was the most beautiful thing
I had heard in months.

***

I started sleeping in my clothes
not long after I got there.
They would wake us up and
give us five minutes to get dressed,
make our bed, and
be back on line,
ready to start the day.
In order to save myself some time in the mornings,
I would sleep in my BDU pants and
blue sweatshirt.
If they allowed us to sleep above the covers,
I would have probably done that too,
but they wouldn't let us.

One night I was laying in my bunk,
under the covers, sleeping.
Two students were messing around,
acting like they were about to try to escape
out of the second story window
by my bunk,
but obviously weren't about to do it.

Down below, by the corner of the building,
our night watch was
watching them from the shadows,
and to him,
it looked like students were
thinking about running.

I woke to my covers being pulled off and a
flashlight in my face.
Then he walked away.
The next morning, the drill instructor
woke us like usual,
but called me out.

While everyone stood on line,
I was ordered to

strip down to my underwear.
Once I was standing there in
front of everyone in my underwear,
the DI threw a bedsheet at me and
ordered me into the bathroom.

I tried explaining that I hadn't done anything,
but I wasn't given permission to speak.

I covered up with the bedsheet and
joined the other kid who was
already in there for
actually attempting to run away.

I felt humiliated and defeated.
Since this facility was better and
didn't have the seminars or points,
I was actually trying to do better.
I had graduated out of eval within a week and
was now in Charley company.
I actually wanted to make the
climb to Alpha company.
But now I was in trouble, and
going to have to start back in eval platoon.

While we were in the bathroom, we weren't
allowed to do anything except
stand with our nose touching the wall.

The only relief we received while we
stood like that was chow time and
when we cleaned the bathroom after
everyone used it in the morning
and at night.

During chow time, another student told me
he was the one by my window, and
let me know he would
talk to the DI for me when he had a chance.
After about fourteen hours of staring at the wall,

the DI finally brought the other kid and I together
and got the whole story.

I was finally relieved and
my clothes were given back to me,
but I have to admit,
it was nice not getting smoked that day
while they were all outside.
If the cadets were smoked inside,
the runaways had to join the fun, but
if they were getting smoked outside,
they were spared.

Part 13

About halfway through the day, a
couple of my friends whispered about a riot
another company was planning.

They said when the other company was ready,
we'd know and to just go along with it.

They couldn't stop us all.

There were only three night guards to about
a hundred and twenty of us.
That was an easy enough plan.

That night, after the DIs had their fill of
making us push,
we waited.

We started to hear the bottom floor
get louder and louder.
And when that happened,
we began to get louder and louder.
Kids started jumping out of their bunks and
around the bay.

The night watch stood up and
started telling us that our DI was
going to have fun with us in the morning,
but we didn't pay any attention to him.

My buddy, Steven and I
noticed the breaker box and
made our way over to it.
Once we opened the panel door,
he reached up
and flipped all the switches,

killing the power in our building.

Right when it went black,
all the windows seemed to
break out of the building simultaneously.
As I backed away from the breaker box,
through the darkness I made out
another friend of mine
picking up one of the
trunks we kept our clothes in, and
throwing it.

I turned around and saw a
group of kids who had
another student in the corner and
they were beating him.

Mattresses, trunks, light fixtures, and
everything the students could think of to
pick up and throw, or break, were
being thrown and broken.

I felt Steven grab me and push me
toward the window next to the
locked side door.
We both climbed through it and
jumped onto the staircase.
We made it to the bottom of the stairs and

bolted for the fence.
Steven made it over the fence first and
I followed.
When I got to the top, I heard,
"Hey, get back here!" from one of the night guards.
I sat on the top of the fence and
slid off,
scratching the backs of both thighs on
the twisted chain link.
I started to run and heard
someone else land behind me;
It was another escapee, Brian.
As Brian, Steven, and I ran down the road,
I told them that we needed to get off the road because
cars were going to be headed this way—
People were going to come because of the riot.

Right after I said that,
we saw headlights appear in front of us and
ran into the field that was to our right.

Then, to our horror,
we saw the farmer's house lights turn on and
saw a truck start up.
We were in this man's field and
didn't know how he was going to take it.
We tried our hardest to make it across the field and
into the jungle.

We knew there were train tracks in the
direction we were going, because we could
hear the train daily, and
our plan was to make it to them.
Then, we were going to walk along the tracks
until a train came and stow away on it.

We ran with everything we had.
We huffed and huffed as the now three trucks
gained and gained.

As we reached the end of the field, we
leaped with everything we had,
only to land right in the farmer's
brush pile he had pushed into the jungle
at the edge of his field.

"What the fuck!?" I screamed.
I was confused.
We clawed and climbed and couldn't figure out
what we were stuck in because it was dark.
Within a second, we were
cornered by the three trucks.
"Alright, let's go,"
one of the farmers ordered us as he stepped out.

We complied without a fight.
We knew what we looked like, and
the townspeople's perception of us.
We were troubled teens.
Gangsters and drug users headed down a
path of self-destruction in their eyes, and
we didn't know if these farmers would use their guns.

The three of us got into the
back of one of the farmer's trucks and
the other two farmers left.
On the way back to the school,
Brian begged and pleaded with the man.
He asked him not to bring us back,
but the man didn't listen.

I pulled my toothbrush I had sharpened
(I know, super cliché.
But we had plastic toothbrushes and tile floors,
so, it was easy to make)
out of my pocket and looked at Brian.

I was ready to use it on the man if it meant
escaping the torture and gaining our freedom.

Brian saw what I had and shook his head at me.

When we got back to the facility,
the police and fire station were there.

The cadets were all still running around
breaking things and
spraying the fire extinguishers.
A few cadets had real cigarettes and
the rest who wanted to smoke
rolled up whatever they could find.

It was complete anarchy.

The top floor of our two-story
barracks building was deemed unlivable.
The toilets were ripped out,
sinks were broken,
bunk beds were destroyed,
cameras were ripped out,
and all the light fixtures were gone.

We had caught wind the state was
coming to investigate Eagle Point, so
our goal was to make the place
look as bad as possible,
and we did.

***

The door burst open and
the lights flipped on.
A drill instructor walked in,
stepping on mattresses and
screaming.

As he walked, he
pushed groggy kids out of the way
as they attempted to stand, and
kicked mattresses out of the center of the bay.

Normally, when a drill instructor walked into a bay,
we would sound off and jump up to stand at the
position of attention on line.
But he had entered and
was moving too quickly for us to
have given him a proper greeting.

"This is the DI highway!" he screamed
as he pointed to the red stripe painted
down the center of the bay floor.

His face looked rugged and
he wore his hair in a high flattop.

"If I catch any of you stepping foot on it,
I will fucking run you over!"

Apparently, this man was the
school's response to our riot
the day prior.

As soon as he introduced himself,
our hearts sank.
We already knew who he was.
Rumors of this particular drill instructor still
floated throughout the school,
even though he hadn't been there

since the name change.

He had worked at the school before,
when it was under its previous name:
Bethel.

Stories circulated about how he
treated students and
what he used to do to them as
forms of punishment.

The first thing he did
was send us outside to make our morning head call.
There weren't enough urinals for us to all get the
job done in the timeframe he wanted,
so, lining us up outside against the fence
was the faster option.
He started a countdown from ten,
and when he reached one, he started
pulling kids away from the fence
as they were still urinating.
Ten seconds was long enough.

He had us form up after our morning routine and
ordered us to start cleaning up around
buildings within the fence;
there was still garbage and debris everywhere
from the riot.

We instantly became rebellious toward the
new, angry drill instructor.

As we walked around with our garbage bags,
we only pretended to pick up the garbage.
We would pick up a handful and then
drop it to pick up another.
That way, it looked like we were working,
but we weren't.

Eventually, the grounds became clean

because some of the kids were actually
doing what was asked of us,
but it took until almost lunchtime.

Our lunch arrived on Styrofoam trays
placed on a table outside the barracks.

Apparently, he caught onto our antics
during the cleanup,
because he called us to formation for lunch,
took a single tray out of the stack,
and flipped the table,
sending our lunches into the dirt.

He pulled a couple of screwdrivers from his pocket and
held them in his hand as he screamed at us.
"I'll stab y'all in the fuckin eye!"
he threatened, because of our shenanigans.

He then stood the table back on its feet,
sat,
and began eating his lunch in front of us.

While still in formation,
Brian used a shard of glass
to make an incision on his wrists.

Because of the series of events over the
last couple days,
there were hired guards all around.
They quickly handcuffed
the sixteen-year-old boy,
and pulled him in front of formation
at the DI's request.

The bleeding boy stood in front of
our formation,
shamed,
accompanied by the angry,
red-faced drill instructor.

"He didn't even do it right! If you wanna
do it right, I'll fucking show ya!"

Then he tripped the bleeding boy,
sending him forward
into the hard packed dirt.
He hit the side of his head and it
bounced awkwardly off the ground.
He wasn't able to
catch himself because his
hands were cuffed behind his back.
Seeing this,
the other students
began yelling obscenities
and screamed at the instructor,
alerting the guards again.

Streams of pepper spray
entered the formation
of teenage students,
causing us to run.
We didn't make it far because
the guards quickly circled us and
ordered us to lie on the ground,
threatening more pepper spray.

Seeing the spectacle put on by the
crazed drill instructor and
our reaction,
they escorted him from the premises,
fearing he would be the reason if
we were to organize again.

The cadets who were in the line of
fire of the pepper spray spent the rest of the day
nursing their eyes,
unable to come in direct contact with the sunlight.
My eyes didn't take a direct hit, so I recovered faster.

***

Shortly after the riot and
the crazy DI incident,
we noticed students being sent away.

It was always a tossup on whether they
were being sent home, or going to
another program.
We were never told what was happening
when a student was called away and
never returned.

One kid I noticed leave in particular,
was the kid who liked to beat other kids
with his cast.

He had gotten into a fight with another student and
broken his hand in the process.
When they gave him a cast for it,
he just treated it like a weapon.
All the kids he fought had checker pattern
bruises on their faces and heads.
When he disappeared, I just assumed he
went somewhere worse.

When fights happened between the cadets,
the DIs would just walk the brawling kids
into the bathroom and
let them fight there because there
were no cameras.

As the kids were leaving,
new instructors started showing up.
Instead of BDUs and T-shirts,
these guys wore blue shirts and khaki shorts.

We also ended up getting new uniforms of
blue shirts and khaki pants.

The new instructors took over completely
after what seemed like couple cf days.

The DIs the school didn't want to fire
were placed in charge of Eval platoon
in their own building.
They got the first trailer closest to the gate.

We still were under the same regiment as before,
but these guys weren't as good at their job as the
DIs were.
It was almost like they were
trying to be hard on us,
but they struggled because
we were already conditioned by the DI's who were
actually in the Marine Corp.

It was a shit show.

***

After a couple of weeks
with the new instructors,
we were told we were going to have to start
attending seminars.

Fuck, I thought to myself,
*This is WWASP. How the fuck
did it follow me here?*

WWASP was an umbrella organization of
independent schools, in the
"Troubled" Teen Industry.
Academy at Ivy Ridge
being one of them. The seminars
were a core component of their "programs."

I couldn't believe it.
This place was worse than Ivy Ridge physically—
The Ridge had no physical demands.
Now they were throwing
mind games on top of the physical torture.

Luckily, I didn't have to sit through
orientation seminar again
because they had my files from the
other program and could see
I had already attended.

So, I had to go to discovery seminar again.

Day one of discovery,
I stood up when they asked
who didn't want to be there;

I was the only one.
"This isn't for me," I said again.

This time I didn't go to a study hall or

intervention because the school hadn't
designated space for these alternatives.
I was able to return to the
rest of the company who wasn't in discovery yet.
Even so, I was frustrated and exhausted.
I couldn't believe I had to deal with those weird,
culty seminars again.

***

I didn't want any part of the new
program Eagle Point had to offer.

While back with my company,
I ended up asking one of the
instructors a simple question,
I can't remember what it was exactly,
but he responded with,
"Are you stupid or something?"
And that was enough for me.
Not only was this guy super out of shape and
in charge of smoking us,
now he insulted me for asking a question.

I spun around and punched one of the
support pillars that stood in the bay as I passed it.
Then I walked straight to the side door of the bay and
kicked it open.
The instructor was right behind me the whole time,
laughing.
I continued walking toward the
eval platoon trailer and about halfway there,
I spun around and yelled,
"Keep laughing, you fat fuck!" And that
finally shut him up.

I wanted to go back to eval because
I was done.
I'd had it.
These instructors were just playing the
roll of the DIs, but poorly.
On top of that,
I was now being forced to go to those
seminars.

Eval was where the new
kids to the program were.
That's where the actual DIs worked now,

but at least I wasn't going to be
forced into those seminars
on top of the physical torment.
I was mentally tired.
I snapped to attention when I
walked through the door.

"This cadet requests permission to speak, sir."
"Speak," the DI replied.
"This cadet requests permission to come back to eval, sir,"
I asked, standing rigid and stoned faced.
"Okay, cadet." He replied.

I was once again free from WWASP
in that little trailer of scared new kids.

***

One day I noticed a little bump
on my leg that looked like a zit.

I popped it, of course,
thinking it was a normal little heat bump
from the Mississippi humidity.

I didn't think anything of it when I did it,
but the next day,
there were two more.
The next day, the same thing happened,
and then the next.

My legs started to swell badly and
I could feel it every time I stood up.
It felt like blood was rushing to my shins
so badly my bones would explode.

One day, they were having us
run to the fence and back because
we kept messing up.

They would make us run to the fence and back
with a time we had to be
back in line and perfectly still by.
If the DI saw movement while we were
standing in line,
he would make us run to the fence again.

We came back in and
I tried with everything I had,
but I was exhausted and
the pain in my legs was unbearable.
I bent forward in agony and
fucked it up for everyone.
We had to run to the fence again.

I tried explaining to the DI that my legs hurt,

but he said they were just bug bites and
to quit "fuckin with 'em."

I ended up making it through the night,
but the next morning it was simply
too painful to walk,
and that's when the nurse finally
came to check on me.

I was finally able to go to the hospital
after a week of this infection spreading
all over my legs.
By the time I made it to the doctor,
both legs were perfectly round like footballs,
and I could barely walk to the door of the office.
Another student who also had an appointment
had to help me to the door.

It turns out I had multiple staph infection
pustules all over my legs from the knee down.
It had spread to my other leg because
they made us sit cross legged
when we sat on line.

Staph and MRSA flourished throughout the facility
because of the conditions.
There were no janitors or crews to
clean the barracks.
That was left to the kids.

I saw sores and pustules on many of the kids,
but I had never seen a reaction like mine,
so, I didn't know what was happening.

***

Eventually, the DIs sent me back to the company.
Eval wasn't meant to be a long-term stay.

I had been back for a couple of weeks when
the instructors called us to attention.
We all stood stone faced as they informed us
we were going to have to evacuate the school
and we didn't have much time.

Hurricane Katrina was moving in.

We all gathered a change of clothes,
our bedding,
and lined up along the fence to
board the bus.

The ride was relatively short.

They decided an old sewing factory warehouse was the
best place for a hundred or so students
to wait the storm out.

There were leftover pallets in the warehouse,
and the instructors decided the
best thing we could do was
lay them out in an orderly fashion
and make them our beds for the night.

As we built our makeshift beds out of the
pallets and our bedsheets,
the weather became worse and worse.

We began hearing sounds of
objects landing on the tin roof
of our structure,
and it became dark.
Even though it was dark,
it remained strangely light enough for us

to see outside,
when we became curious and
opened the big sliding door
enough for us to take a peek.

I had never seen anything like it before,
being raised in California.

As we stood and watched,
branches bigger than I could lift blew by the door
and were ripped from the trees.
Thunder clashed and lightning lit up the
thick, dark clouds that blackened the sky.
Surges of wind and rain carried large pieces of debris
through the air.

It was spectacular.

I had never witnessed the true forces of nature.
The ominous sounds of the storm and power it held
were remarkable.

As we tried to sleep that night,
we woke to water creeping in under us.
A corner of the roof had ripped off in another
section of the warehouse and
rainwater was flooding the building.
Lucky for us,
we were raised off the floor by our
pallet beds.

In the morning, after the storm had passed,
we were bussed back to the campus.
On the way there we all spoke quietly,
hoping the school had been destroyed.

That was too good to be true,
of course.

We arrived back at the school and

filed off the bus,
only to find the
school in better shape than the warehouse
we had sought refuge in was.

The fence was blown over and
out of the three buildings. There was only
one broken window.

The storm had not freed us.

***

A couple of days after the hurricane,
I was called out of formation by my family rep.
It was time for my monthly phone call.
The facility hadn't been completely
taken over by WWASP yet,
so we still received a phone call with our
parents once a month.

Phone calls happened the same way here as
they did when you reached level three at the Ridge.
If you damned the school, the family rep would
hang the phone up.

During the phone call, my dad
surprised me with a question.

"Do you want to go to Jamaica,
or do you want to come home?"

Tears welled in my eyes,
but I actually thought about it for a second.

Did I want to go back to him,
or go to another facility that was
deemed to be the worst?
If you ended up going through
Ivy Ridge and Eagle Point,
Tranquility Bay was the next step.

Because I thought it might be worse and
I didn't know what could happen to me
in a developing country,
I replied with,

"I wanna come home."

Part 14

O n the way home from the airport,
we stopped at a Denny's for some lunch.
Mom and Dad both came to pick me up,
which I found odd.

Normally, during the day, Father was working and
Mother would be the one to
cart kids around if they needed it.

While we were sitting at the table,
Mom asked me if my
muscles had gotten any bigger from the
boot camp, and I showed her.

Father asked how many pushups I could do and
I replied with,
"As many as you want."

Then, Mom asked what it was like there.

I started explaining our daily routine,
but she stopped me,

saying that she didn't want to hear
anything bad about the program.
I knew they weren't going to
accept anything negative I said
about the program,
so I was already trying to avoid it.

I don't even remember what I said to
trigger her to cut me off,
but she did.

During our meal, Father laid down some new
ground rules he wanted me to abide by:
1. No phone calls with Mother. I was allowed to write to her, but that was it.
2. I wasn't allowed to wear the clothes I wanted to wear. He had to approve of them.
3. No more metal music.
4. I have to pass all of my classes.

When we got home,
Father went right back to work, and
I went to my room.

I sat and stared at the wall for
what seemed like forever.
I didn't know what to do.
For the last year, someone had
dictated my every move.

I felt like I was supposed to be
doing something,
but I didn't know what to do.
I felt like I might get in trouble because
I was supposed to be doing something,
but didn't know what to do.
I felt nervousness and anxiety
in my chest and throat.

Eventually, I stood up and walked to my door
to peer over the balcony to see

if anyone was downstairs.

I noticed the sunshine coming
in through the window on the carpet;
it looked warm,
soft,
inviting…

"Why don't you get ready for dinner?"
Mom called up from the kitchen.
Her voice startled me, snapping me
out of my daze.

***

My dad took me clothes shopping
the weekend before I was to
start back at my old high school.

While we were on our way to
take me shopping, he was on the
phone with someone.
The person on the phone was
surprised to learn I was home,
and he explained to them that I
wasn't home because I was "cured,"
and that I was brought home for
another reason.

He picked out five different collared shirts
and three pairs of pants for me.
I knew if I complained about the
style of clothing, it would be all for naught,
so I didn't say anything,
but I hated them.

Fancy, twenty-five-dollar name brand shirts
were not my thing;
I wanted my Korn and Slipknot shirts back
that Mother had bought for me.

I only ever hung out with a group of
two or three people.
The friends I had when I left had split up and
were hanging out with other people I didn't know.
Of course, they introduced me to the
new friends they had made in my absence,
but I wasn't too fond of them.
I didn't know them on a personal level like I did
my friends I'd known since middle and elementary school, so
it felt weird to hang out with these strangers.

My school never felt homey and

I never liked it much,
and now it was like when I left,
my friends moved on without me.
I couldn't blame them, though.

I disappeared out of thin air
a whole year ago.

A couple of my teachers kept having to remind me
not to call them sir and ma'am
because I was still in the habit from Eagle Point.
Some didn't mind
because I probably sounded like the most polite kid
they had ever spoken to.

After my first day back, I started using my friend's
cell phone to call my mother every morning.
That was a rule Father made that
I didn't think was fair to myself or her.

Then it took me a couple days of
wandering around the house while Mom and Dad were out
for me to locate Nathan's old CDs.
They weren't metal, which I preferred,
but they were better than nothing.
I could do Pearl Jam and Green Day
instead of country or pop.

Within a week, I was hiding normal
T-shirts in my backpack and changing into them
when I got to school;
They weren't my metal shirts,
but at least they weren't those
fancy collared bullshits that Father was
trying to get me to wear.

I was breaking every rule except the one about school,
because I didn't feel they were right.

Why couldn't I listen to the music I wanted to listen to,

call my mother, and
wear what I wanted to wear,
as long as I managed to keep my grades up?
I didn't see how any of those things mattered
because they had
nothing to do with my academic performance.

***

One day after school, I was
sitting at the kitchen table talking to Mom
while she prepared dinner.

I always spoke to her like a friend because
she was picky and choosy with
what she did and did not tell Father.

Most of the time, if it was something simple
that she agreed with me on,
she wouldn't relay it to him.

This time, I told on myself about
all the things I had been doing and
instead of telling Father herself,
she told me I should tell him.

That night after dinner we were all sitting,
watching TV, and Mom said,

"Your son has something to tell you."

To my surprise,
Father turned off the TV and
asked me what was up.
Normally, he never turned the
TV off to talk to me.

"Well, I've been calling my mom
every day from school on my friends
cell phone,
listening to Nathan's old CDs, and
changing my shirt every day at school."

"God damnit!" Father yelled and
slammed down the newspaper
he was reading.

He stood up and started walking toward his office.
Before he got there,
he turned around and said,
"I don't know how you can be
so fucking deceitful."
He then ordered me to my room.

I didn't know what the word "deceitful"
meant at the time,
so I didn't reply to him.

I got up from the couch and
started walking up the stairs to my room.
I reached the top of the stairs and
Father emerged from his office yelling about
how he had tried everything and
didn't understand
why I was the way I was.
"You were never easy,"
was one of the phrases he used.

Eventually, I cut him off.
"I'm about to be seventeen in a month.
I'm not going to graduate here anyway
because as soon as I turn eighteen, I'm leaving.
I still don't want to be here.
Keeping me here doesn't make any sense."

While I was saying all of that,
I noticed that even though he was yelling and
screaming,
I was able to maintain my composure.
I was speaking calmly, coolly, and collectively
while he was
pacing around and yelling like a madman.

After a brief pause, he replied with,
"Fine, go."

My heart jumped.

"Are you serious?" I asked.
"Ya. You can go tomorrow. I'm done."

I was ecstatic,
but I didn't know how to respond,
so I just turned around and went into my room.
I sat on the bed a minute with
tears running down my face, and
then I picked up my phone to dial
Mother's number.

"I wanna come home, Mama,"
I said as I sniffled into the phone.
"Okay, baby."
"I'm coming home."
"Okay, baby," she said again.

Mother never had to question me,
no matter how cryptic I was.
She understood what was happening, and
she welcomed me with open arms.
We had both wanted this moment since
the beginning.

After I hung up the phone, Mother received another call.

"I'm sending Colin to you."
"Okay," Mother replied.
"I'm not sending you any money," Father said sternly.
"That's fine," Mother said.

Mother was never one to worry about money.
She would always "figure it out"
when times were rough, and
this didn't change anything.

The next day, Mom took me to the
Greyhound station with nothing but a backpack that
had the few things I cared for in it. After all these years,
I was finally set free.

Part 15

Mother took me to my old high school in Reno to enroll me. After filling out the paperwork, we sat in the office while my schedule was put together.

The school informed us that nothing I had done at the Academy at Ivy Ridge or Eagle Point Christian Academy counted.

Neither were accredited schools. Schools that cost my father $3,000 a month and I had nothing to show for it.

At this point, I was about to be a junior with barely any freshman credits.

Mother sighed heavily. "God damn it," she said.

I was saddened and angry at the same time.
It seemed like there was so much I had to do
to make up for all the lost schooling.
In my sixteen-year-old brain it seemed like
my diploma was sitting on top of Mt. Everest.

Even so,
I thought since I was at the tail end of my
sophomore year,
I could buckle down and
make up the time I had lost at the facilities,
with an alternative education class, the school offered, and
summer school in between my remaining school years.

So, that was the goal I set for myself...

Epilogue

"Hello," my father's voice, on the other line of the phone.
"Hey Dad."
"What's up?"
"I got married, my wife is pregnant, and I'm joining the army."
"Well okay. That's good."
"I just wanted to call and let you know."

Thank you for your purchase. If you would like to know more about the programs/facilities mentioned in this book, please watch

The Program: Cons, Cults, and Kidnapping

on Netflix.

Thank you for reading.

ABOUT THE AUTHOR

Colin Buckley is a two-time combat veteran, father, husband, and artist. Colin's varied life experiences, including being adopted at birth, two tours overseas in Iraq and Afghanistan, becoming a truck driver, farming, and raising his four kids, have given him a sincere and shockingly raw voice behind his work. When Colin isn't busy navigating the complexities of being a stay-at-home dad and husband, he enjoys billiards, skateboarding, and traveling with his family.

www.ingramcontent.com/pod-product-compliance
Lightning Source LLC
LaVergne TN
LVHW011326080426
835513LV00006B/215